Praise for Dr. Judith Segal's

GETTING THEM TO SEE IT YOUR WAY

"This is not your usual, tedious, run-of-the-mill self-help book. Dr. Segal writes with charm and a playful intelligence that makes learning these valuable communication skills fun. Instead of dreading my next confrontation, I'm looking forward to it."

—*Larry Wray, Senior Recruiter, Glendale Memorial Hospital & Health Center*

"Valuable advice on how to simplify the most challenging problems. It's fun and it works."

—*Karen Heller, Director of Employee Development
and Administration, OOCL (USA) Inc.*

"The most successful tools I have ever used in bringing diverse groups of people with very differing agendas together and on a path to common growth. I recommend not only reading and absorbing this book, but also living it in all aspects of your life. You will never be the same!"

—*Michael Hawkins, past president, California Restaurant Association*

"Direct, straightforward, and full of practical advice. I always wanted a how-to instruction manual on dealing with difficult people, and this is it."

—*Richard R. Frank, President and CEO, Lawry's Restaurants Inc.*

"Dr. Segal's advice is always provocative, creative, and practical. She has a lot of insight because of the breadth of her experience. . . . This is good, sound advice. She is always tough and challenging; she doesn't sugar-coat it."

—*Pat McIntyre, COO, Pure Fishing*

"Dr. Segal's ability to teach people how to read people creates immeasurable added value."

—*Howard Fink, Managing Partner, Fink & Company, LLP*

"Straight shooting from one of the best."

—*Mark Foster, President, Condit Exhibits*

Getting Them to See It Your Way probes ones of the immutable facts of life—the world is full of difficult people and in order to be successful in our lives we must learn how to deal with them. With a remarkable insight and candor, Dr. Segal gives us the tools to gain control over one of the key aspects of our lives—our relationships with difficult people."

—*Catherine Osler, President, Titian Communications Inc.*

GETTING THEM
TO SEE
IT YOUR WAY

DEALING WITH DIFFICULT
AND CHALLENGING PEOPLE

JUDITH SEGAL, PH.D.

LOWELL HOUSE

LOS ANGELES

NTC/Contemporary Publishing Group

Library of Congress Cataloging-in-Publication Data

Segal, Judith, Ph.D.
　　Getting them to see it your way: dealing with difficult and
　　challenging people / Judith Segal.
　　　　p. cm.
　　Includes index.
　　ISBN 0-7373-0377 (alk.)
　　1. Conflict management. 2. Interpersonal communication.
　　3. Interpersonal relations. I. Title.

　　HM1126.S44 2000　　　　　　　　　　　　　　　99-056447
　　303.6'9—dc21

Published by Lowell House
A division of NTC/Contemporary Publishing Group, Inc.
4255 West Touhy Avenue, Lincolnwood, Illinois 60646-1975 U.S.A.

Interior design by Cheryl Carrington

Printed in the United States of America
International Standard Book Number: 0-7373-0377-8
00 01 02 03 04 DHD 18 17 16 15 14 13 12 11 10 9 8 7 6 5 4 3 2 1

CONTENTS

ACKNOWLEDGMENTS

I would like to express my appreciation to the many people who have been so generous with their time, feedback, and information: Judith B. Davis, Teri Donnelly, Mimi Grabis, Peter Gray, Karen Heller, Patricia Howard, Shel Katzer, Melanie King, Ellen Lachtman, Richard McDonald, Robert Nagge, Deborah Pinsky, Susan Salenger, and Dianne Wehner. I would especially like to thank Dr. Robert Crook for all his help, advice, and support. Most of all, I want to acknowledge my husband, Wayne Litwin, for contributing so much and always with honesty, humor, and insight.

THE GETTING-
THEM TO-SEE-
IT-YOUR-WAY
CHALLENGE

eople tell me the same stories over and over again: They complain about obnoxious, inappropriate, and seemingly unconscious people who are difficult to deal with. Some of these frustrated individuals have stubborn family members with unrealistic expectations; others resent having to "baby-sit" people they manage at work; some complain about people who are abrasive, closed minded, or "shut down" and, as such, unwilling to engage in positive discussions. All say the same thing: Some of these problem people are so difficult that they threaten to interfere with or destroy careers or family life. Most people who approach me think there is nothing that can be done about situations such as these, yet I know this isn't true. There is something that can be done. It is possible to learn how to turn things around. It is possible to get people to see things your way. *Getting Them to See It Your Way* is about learning how to effectively deal with people who are difficult in all facets of your life—people who either don't want to hear or acknowledge your position in a given situation, are unwilling to give your position any merit, or fight aggressively to discount or eliminate a position other than their own for whatever reason.

You opened this book because the title hit home for you. You may be at the level you want to be in your interpersonal relationships, making progress but not as quickly as you might like. Or, you might be hanging on by your fingertips because you feel like you are going nowhere or sliding backward and losing ground rapidly. Perhaps you thought of the challenging people in your life, past and present, and were interested in possible options for turning these relationships around.

Let me tell you, up front, that reading this book will help you take a giant step toward developing the skills you'll need to do what must be done: not to resent the individuals who are giving you difficulty but, on the contrary, to learn how to deal with the difficult ones effectively and, in so doing, allow yourself to appreciate and really enjoy the "good" ones.

This book is geared toward helping you to have open lines of communication and more successful dealings with people who are "normal neurotics," not pathological deviants, in your personal and work lives. If the people you are trying to influence are verbally or emotionally abusive in any way, your first action should always be to decide whether it is worth your while to try to engage them in any kind of meaningful interaction. Sometimes it is, and sometimes it isn't. Feeling frustrated or undervalued is one thing; feeling destroyed is another. It is not always worth it to try to change the situation. Sometimes, the best decision you can make is to decide that it is better to cut your losses and move on.

Dealing with stressed, confused, manipulative, and, in some cases, seemingly unconscious people takes skill, knowledge, experience, and resilience. What you say and the way you say it to them are important. The way you feel about yourself before, during, and after is crucial. Ask yourself whether you feel powerful or powerless, exhausted or energized in your relationships with challenging people. Ask yourself how much time you waste getting nowhere. Are you where you want to be or still working on getting there? Is "there" anywhere in sight?

Face it. You can't get cantankerous people to stop behaving badly without learning how to position yourself so that you're strong without creating even more hostility or resentment (but not at their expense), assertive without being overly manipulative or subversive, and direct without being overbearing. Dumping on difficult, challenging, and resistant people is not the answer. Changing the rules and your tactics so that they can't dump on you is.

You can learn to stay in control of yourself, to package yourself to be "tamperproof." You can learn to take care of yourself and take care of business at the same time. You can learn to stand your ground and feel confident and in control enough to talk to any challenging individual at any time about anything you choose without feeling as if you are beating your head against a brick wall.

What makes the people in your life difficult? I have found that such people seem to have three characteristics in common. First, they are in some way communicatively challenged. Whether they are hiding their opinions or feelings or pushing them on you with great intensity, their communication is not clear, open, or direct, and it is usually dishonest. Second, whether they are totally withholding of their feelings, totally unaware that they even have feelings, or out of control and blasting their feelings, they are emotionally challenged. If they have any emotions at all, they hide them well, are ruled by them, or are totally out of touch with them. And last but not least, they are control freaks. Whether they control you with their passive behavior or their bluntly aggressive acting-out, they all show signs of needing to control, which makes them relationship-challenged.

Regardless of the reasons, what matters is that you learn to deal with them. It's not practical to waste time wondering or lashing out when you could be on your way to changing things and enjoying success. You need to gain the perspective, confidence, edge, and communication skills that will put you in control of yourself and your situation. You need to adjust your thinking so that you stop acting and feeling like a renegade or a victim. You need to arm yourself with the reactions and the words that will get you through those tough situations with anyone who doesn't want to see it your way.

THE GETTING-THEM-TO-SEE-IT-YOUR-WAY PLAN

This book will equip you with the tools you need to make the changes you want with the people in your life who refuse to see it your way or refuse to acknowledge that your way even exists.

Here is the game plan. In order to reduce or overcome the resistance you face, you first must understand and acknowledge exactly what the situation is, how it got to be this way, and what you knowingly or unknowingly do to perpetuate it. You do have some responsibility, and you have to own up to it if you want to make things more effective and productive for yourself. Chapter 1 will cover these dynamics and will detail how to recognize a severe, if yet undiagnosed, case of Deference Syndrome. You'll also get a chance to understand the myth of abrasive power and how it holds us back. Once you understand where you are and how you got here, your next step will be to assess the difficult people you have to deal with in all aspects of your life. You may keep on attracting different types of resistant people, or you may find the same type over and over again. The "Are You a Difficult-Person Magnet?" quiz on page 18 will quickly allow you to identify whom you're attracting and whether your condition is "localized."

In chapter 2, you'll look at some specific reasons why you are encountering and having difficulty influencing those people. You'll begin to examine the different types of difficult people in all areas of your life, from the Blamer and the Destroyer to the Victim and the Spoiled Brat, with many others in between. You'll look at who they are, what makes them tick, and what makes them keep on ticking. You'll go right to the heart of the issue, looking at specific words and behaviors to use with the different types of antagonists who are making unwelcome and challenging appearances in your life. If you want a choice of techniques to choose from, this is where you can get it. After you've read this chapter, your rapid response diagnostic tools will be in place, and such individuals won't stand a chance; they'll be totally exposed to you for who and what they are.

Chapter 3, the attitude-adjustment chapter, will take you through all the moves you have to make to effectively improve troublesome relationships. It will give you the clarity that will help you decide to change the way people respond to you. You can stop wasting precious time, energy, and resources worrying about what others think and start focusing on what you want to accomplish.

You will begin at the beginning, examining and adjusting your attitude, because if you focus on results, you'll get results. If you expect someone to see things your way, you'll do whatever you need to do to make it happen. Once you've adjusted your attitude, you'll be ready to go into a change mode. If you were going on a rock-climbing expedition, you'd have to psych yourself up, get the right equipment, and learn some basic techniques. What you are doing here is no different. Once you've got your self-talk sounding better, you've got to work on how you approach and talk to people who don't want to see things your way. Whether you are a power player now or an up-and-coming power player, this chapter will make a tremendous difference in the way you look at the challenges that you and others around you are facing.

Chapter 4 will arm you with the appropriate skills for implementing change. You will be prepared to appropriately and constructively confront any person who does not want to see a situation your way. You'll get the tools you need to get started on breaking your old, damaging habits, even the ones you don't yet realize are working against you.

Then it's on to chapter 5, a step-by-step guide to conflict savvy, where you will make sure that your strategy and timing are properly set and that you are perfectly ready to go from start to finish, with no questions and problems in between. You won't have to waste time or energy. You will be able to do something, do it right, get what you want, and then move on and forget about it. Here you will take time out for a reality check to ensure that you are taking on opponents only when it is worth it to you to engage with them and when you have a chance of being successful.

Chapter 6 is about backlash and coping with negative reactions. This will be very important, so don't stop before you get there. This is where you will focus on what happens when you change your behavior and begin to go after what you want. You will learn how to anticipate the negative reactions you may encounter. This chapter will give you some directions on how to formulate plans for when negative backlash occurs and your nemeses, if you will, launch a counterattack or instigate counter maneuvers.

Are you part of the "difficult and challenging people" problem in your work life . . . or the solution?

The key to dealing with difficult and challenging people is to look at each of them as a potential growth experience, another experiment in your trial-and-error method of taking control of yourself and your relationships.

When you are dealing with difficult people who don't want to see it your way, do you

1. Immediately assume a caring role?
2. Convince yourself that if you do confront them, you'll probably lose?
3. Worry about them not liking you?
4. Tend to become too aggressive?
5. Automatically take a subservient position?
6. Act like a victim when you don't get your way?
7. Use pouting and withdrawing to soften them up?
8. Run hot and cold, being inconsistent with your reactions?
9. Worry that other people will blame you for any upheaval?
10. Never ask for what you want?

When you are honest with yourself and acknowledge that you have some or many of these nonproductive habits, you will already be on the road to getting them to see it your way.

Finally, chapter 7 will describe how to deal with success and enjoy new types of influential relationships with people who are no longer resistant to seeing things your way. It will help you cement your new skills and keep you from backsliding.

While reading this you may be talking to yourself and doing a good job of convincing yourself that your situation is impossible and will never change or that it is not worth the effort, will never stick, or will take too long to really get better. You may be struggling with the notion that you might as well just learn to live with things the way they are. If this description fits you, then you really need this chapter because it will help you to realize there is always a different way to approach a tough person or situation. It will remind you that sometimes the most important thing you can do is adjust your expectations. The possibilities are endless, and so are the opportunities.

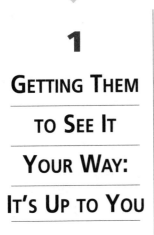

1

GETTING THEM
TO SEE IT
YOUR WAY:
IT'S UP TO YOU

The key to dealing with people who don't want to see things your way is to look at each difficult person and situation as a potential growth experience, an experiment in your trial-and-error process of changing the way people see you and what you have to offer. I don't think that I know of one person who has not had to deal with a difficult individual at some point in his or her life. In fact, a lot of the people I coach seem to function as magnets for difficult people.

Have you noticed this, and have you also noticed that the same person can be difficult with some people and not with others? You have to ask yourself how this happens, and, when you do that, you have to take some responsibility for those individuals continuing to be the way they are with you.

Although not all people are difficult, enough of them are to warrant some serious attention. Some of the people you might find the most challenging don't mean to be difficult, and some are amazed when it is suggested to them that they are being resistant. When confronted, they look at you with disbelief.

Ask anybody what makes people difficult and biased toward what you bring to the table and you'll get similar answers:

> They have preconceived notions about their roles, and, as a result, they feel threatened by any ideas other than their own.
>
> They equate being difficult with strength and leadership. They believe they're supposed to be this way because their position demands it.
>
> They're insecure about everything and are afraid that you will make them look bad. They have already formed an opinion of you and are convinced that nothing you have to say has any merit or value.

Even though you may understand what they are doing and you know how it makes you feel, you still may be tolerant because, for one reason or another, you don't think you can change the situation or you don't think you should risk it. Many people with whom I've spoken say the same thing about the dilemma:

> Most of the time, when someone is being difficult, others around that person allow it. In fact, they often

accept it and reinforce it by being unwilling to say, "Knock it off!"

With coworkers, too often others promote difficult behavior by working more on an emotional level, personalizing things or sounding gushy by saying things like "I feel" instead of "I want."

People don't change because you want them to, and they don't even change because you think they should. They change because they decide that it is appropriate, that there is something in it for them, or that their old behavior no longer works. An old saying goes, "You can't teach a pig to sing; you waste your time and annoy the pig." To get difficult or resistant people to sing, you have to make them want to sing.

When someone at the office is creating problems, coworkers often turn them into emotional issues and unknowingly make the situation worse by trivializing their own feelings. This then makes it possible for the difficult person to dismiss coworkers as whining, complaining, and overreacting. One can actually help difficult people cement their old, dysfunctional ways of acting by overlooking the miserable things they do. Well, enough is enough. It is not up to them to decide to change when they feel like it. A lot of people will never feel like it, and why should they? Life is good. People defer. Things are just dandy for them, thank you very much.

Be different. Make a deal with yourself. This process of dealing with difficult people who don't want to see things your way is not about outsmarting them at their own game or acting like Attila the Hun. The changes that need to happen are in you. You put up the barriers to personal success, and you can take them down. When you see a difficult person approaching, try something new. Roll up the red carpet and take out the microscope instead. Put the difficult person on a slide and take a good look to understand what you're dealing with, then put yourself on the same slide and really examine your part and work on yourself. In other words, acknowledge his or her behavior but focus on your own.

GENDER ISSUES IN RELATIONSHIPS

Difficult relationships in which people don't see things your way are often a result of gender differences, about which much has been written. Many girls grow up deferring to boys. They value boys more than other girls. In school, teachers always look to boys for the right answers. Boys are expected to take more risks, be more independent, look after themselves, and look after girls. Many grow up believing that they are hot stuff. After I completed my master's degree, I became interested in what made women act the way they did with each other and with men. For years, when I taught graduate courses in human sexuality to therapists, clergy, nurses, police, and other groups, I asked the women in my classes to list the messages that they got about "how girls and women are" and "how boys and men should be" and asked the men to do the same thing in reverse: to write down "how men and boys are" and "how girls and women should be." Regardless of the classes, the lists were almost always identical.

This is what the women said:

Girls and women are

Money spenders, not moneymakers
Here to make people happy
Supposed to smile
Emotional
Sexual—but not too sexual
Supposed to say "thank you"
Not supposed to talk back
Supposed to be prudish until
   they get married and then
   only a little bit prudish
Not supposed to get angry
Not supposed to let boys know
   that they're smart
Not supposed to ask too many
   questions

Bad drivers
Soft
Always dieting
Naïve
Self-conscious
Fickle
Temperamental
Ignorant
Usable
Jealous
Mothers
Inexperienced
Hard to understand

Boys and men should be

Superior to women
Stronger
Smarter
Better drivers
Coordinated
Confident
Breadwinners
Financially secure
Taller
Dominant
Always on top

Presidents
Politically aggressive
Doctors
Lawyers
Demanding
Masculine
Cool
Sophisticated
With-it
Sly
Clever

This is what the men said:

Boys and men are	
Rough	Possessive
Tough	Athletic
Strong	Mechanically inclined
Insensitive	Domineering
Selfish	Breadwinners
Egotistical	Unfaithful
Unemotional	Vain
Competitive	Uncaring

Girls and women should be	
Shorter than boys	Poised
Respectable	Mothers
Soft-spoken	Less trustworthy
Naïve	Subservient
Graceful	Ladies
Feminine	Clean
Slim	Good cooks
Maternal	Patient
Faithful	Creative

Isn't it amazing—and horrifying? Afternoon TV talk shows demonstrate that although some progress has been made, many people are still stuck in limiting and often damaging gender camps. So much damage has been done on both sides. Just comparing the two lists gives a very clear picture of how people's upbringings have often worked against them and how these perceptions have influenced they way they interact with others in all aspects of their lives. Many women still allow men to be difficult because they bought the myth and don't think they have a right to anything different; many men still do the very same thing with women, at work and at home.

Most women who have gone through my sexuality or management seminars have one thing in common: For some portion of their lives, beginning in childhood, they believed that it was their sole job to make men happy, to gain approval from men, and to defer to men. A significant number believed that it was inappropriate to outwardly demand anything from men and that they ought to feel grateful to have a man, any man. When they believe these things, they automatically give difficult men permission to be so and deprive themselves of the ability to assert their wants and needs.

Men, on the other hand, having been brought up with their own myths, still believe that they ought to be in control and the decision makers whether they want to be or not. Many men see themselves as "always drivers, never passengers."

Even though a lot of women have made it to middle and upper management, there are still many unresolved gender issues in the workplace. Many women don't want to work for other women, and many men don't want to work for women either. Some women are overly aggressive, saying that it is the only way for them to survive. Sometimes, people use the gender issue as an excuse, and they attribute a difference of opinion to gender differences instead of to the fact that these are two people with two different points of view. Men are supposed to be dynamic leaders, yet they are also supposed to be in touch with their feelings. There is still the expectation that men will use facts and women will use feelings when it comes to solving problems. It is not unusual for people to highlight the exception when the opposite occurs.

Keep in mind that these ideas and beliefs have been chiseled into people's minds, bodies, and beings since day one. If you are a woman, think about yourself. Do you believe that you have to refrain from asking questions, either because they'll make you look too smart or too stupid? I cannot tell you how many times women in my seminars begin their questions by saying, "This is probably a stupid question, but . . . ?

Ask yourself if you believe that it's okay to say no, or that saying no will make you seem rude and inconsiderate. Do you believe that if people around you are miserable, you should have done, or are supposed to do, something to make them feel better? Can you relate to the idea that you should not tell the truth if it means that you might hurt someone's feelings? If your answer to these questions is yes, then the way you were raised may be interfering with your ability to get others to see things your way.

If you are a man, do you believe that you always have to show confidence, the ability to deal only with facts and not feelings, ask intelligent questions, and come off strong and competitive? Do you feel frustrated when it is assumed that you are not interested in your coworkers? Do you find yourself going head-to-head with highly aggressive people even when you would prefer to back down? If so, then the way you were raised might also be interfering with your ability to get others to see things your way.

Generational differences, like gender differences, can cause one person to ignore, dismiss, or refuse to see another's perspective. One generation tends to look for security and the other, opportunities. It is not unusual to hear a more experienced, older person advising a younger one to hold on to a job because the benefits are good and the retirement package is hard to beat. To a twenty-something-year-old, this is usually of little or no value, and the older worker is seen as a fossil who doesn't understand what is really important. If you are the older person, you probably perceive the younger person to be reckless and not as committed to the job as he or she should be. If you are the younger person, you probably think that the older person is making judgments based on fear and is unwilling to take risks. Based on these differences, it is tough for either person to convince the other of anything on any topic because of the already clearly defined differences.

Other gaps include communication and work styles. One person might be very communicative, finding that working with other people is more beneficial and enjoyable than working alone. This person gets excited at the thought of working as part of a team. To the other person, being assigned to a team, where he actually has to work, collaborate, and communicate with other people throughout the duration of a project, is like a life sentence, and the resentment shows in the form of resistance to others' ideas.

There are many other differences, and one that is particularly noteworthy is the way people choose to avoid or handle conflict. If you like to confront conflict head-on, you might find it particularly frustrating to try to get people to see things your way if they will not even acknowledge that the two of you have any sort of disagreement. One of you may be a yeller and the other a pouter or evidence-gatherer. One of you might prefer to deal with problems as they arise, and the other might prefer to wait until you calm down. Regardless of your preference, the end result is your inability to get the other person to see things your way.

THE DEFERENCE SYNDROME

When George was reporting to Allan, the operations manager, he deferred a lot and, in his own mind, abdicated responsibility, and then blamed Allan for him not getting what he wanted. George helped Allan to be more difficult. He colluded—unknowingly and unintentionally. The following is an example of what George used to do. A customer placed an order for a certain material that would meet precise specs. When George discovered that the material was back-ordered, he told his manager (Allan) that he was going to ask the salesperson to notify the customer that there would be a two-week delay in shipping the order. Allan nearly hit the roof; he told George not to tell the salesperson to call the customer but instead to send him an in-stock material that would be close to what he had ordered. George knew that the customer would not accept this but doubted his position and his ability to reason with or otherwise persuade Allan. But the major reason that George would not try to get Allan to see things his way was because Allan was the boss and George didn't think it his place to challenge him. In his mind, there was no middle ground between complying and confronting.

This brings up something that I will tell you more about later in the book. George should have asked himself when this happened: Do I have a chance of changing Allan's mind? His sense was that there was "No way." Did he want to try to change Allan's mind? Not on your life. He was afraid that not showing deference would cost him his job. In fact, when the whole situation blew up, Allan made his life miserable and told George that he should have given him more information. Because George thought his chance of changing Allan's mind was very slim, he was unwilling to step out of his perceived ranking on the corporate food chain.

Here is a preview of one of my tips to you. George should have at least attempted to engage Allan because

1. He might have won.
2. He did care.
3. He was ready with information.

Think about all the different ways that workers defer to their bosses. Another example is Barbara's "deference" work relationship she had with a difficult professional associate:

> In front of the client, my associate was questioning me about things that he should have known. Why was he doing it? To test me? Well, that was partially right. He was also doing it to establish control and superiority. And the client responded just as he wanted her to. She addressed all subsequent questions and comments to him and totally ignored me. I just sat there and let it happen. I deferred and I resented him for what he did.

Jane and Sarah had been best friends for a long time. When they went on vacations together, Jane always chose places that Sarah didn't really want to go to because they were more expensive than those Sarah would have chosen. When she indicated that she would prefer another place, Jane would roll her eyes, shake her head, laugh at her, and tell her that if she kept thinking of herself as poor, she would always just be "poor little Sarah." Because Jane had a lot more money, Sarah felt uncomfortable asserting herself and believed that Jane was more important and certainly more sophisticated about these things. She deferred to Jane because Jane ridiculed her and embarrassed her into doing things she didn't want to do. This whole situation changed when Sarah got her American Express bill and realized that because of all the money she had just spent on a vacation that she didn't enjoy, she would not have enough money to go home for Thanksgiving. At this point Sarah told Jane that from that point on, even though Jane probably knew more about "in" spots for vacations, she was only willing to go to places that would not force her to sacrifice other things that were important to her. As soon as Sarah stopped deferring, the relationship changed. Jane realized that if she wanted to spend time with Sarah, she had to be open to her suggestions and show her respect.

Let's take a closer look at Deference Syndrome so that you can discover whether or not you suffer from it. Don't worry if you do, since it is curable. Most people have at least a mild case of it—in fact, it's likely if you were raised in North America. June and Ward Cleaver in "Leave It to Beaver" modeled it, and Jim and Margaret Anderson in "Father Knows Best" made it an art form. Ozzie and Harriet brought it to new heights, and let's not even bring up "The Brady Bunch."

Deference Syndrome is most likely to rear its ugly head during conversations with those people you presume to have more knowledge, experience, prestige, or positional power than you do. Perhaps you appear to have less power because you don't sound as authoritative as other people, or don't present your ideas as law.

In terms of gender, it is amazing how often people assume that it is the man who has the powerful position. For example, when Sue has a dinner meeting with her clients and calls a restaurant to make a reservation, the conversation often goes like this:

Sue: I'd like a reservation for two at 7:30 tonight.

Maître d': Of course. What is the name?

Sue: Dr. Jones.

Maître d': Thank you. That's tonight, for two, at 7:30. Please tell Dr. Jones that his table will be ready.

Status often goes a long way in getting people to see things your way, if you are the one who has the status. If the other person has the status, it is very important not to defer.

Do a quick Deference Syndrome spot-check. Do you:

- Pay more attention to what a man says than you do to what a woman says?
- Worry about what older people think in order not to offend them with your suggestions?
- Look more at men than at women when you are talking to both at the same time?
- Worry about what people will think of you?
- Take more time and care to prepare to see someone you think is more important than you?
- Always take the advice of others, even though you know you are right?
- Give in more easily to people who are more experienced or older?
- Believe that you always have to try to please others?
- Put aside what you think and accept what others think?
- Shrug your shoulders when you disagree and don't want to answer a question because you think that your answer would be disrespectful?
- Raise the tone of your voice or blush when confronted?

If your answer is yes to at least three of these, you've been afflicted, and the offending microbe is the Deference Syndrome.

Deference Syndrome usually isn't terminal and it doesn't mean you're stupid, but it can inflict a lot of pain and anguish, and millions of people suffer from it. For some reason, many people grow up thinking that those who have power over them are more important than their own knowledge, experience, or common sense. They ignore their own thoughts, discount the mind, and defer to the most controlling or manipulative type of person even if they know that person is wrong.

And to think that all this starts when people are really young. You might remember a time when one of your peers laughed at you because you couldn't do something very well. This same feeling of humiliation often carries through to adult life and rears its head at the most inopportune times, such as when you are about to make an important presentation and one of your associates ridicules you for not having included some piece of audiovisual data that he said he would have prepared had he been in charge.

If you were raised to always respect your elders, regardless of their behavior or lack of morals, values, or knowledge, the people who raised you did you a disservice in some ways. They didn't make sure that you knew that you not only had the ability to recognize inappropriate behavior but also that it was your responsibility to do so. If this applies to you, how does it affect you today in terms of how you function, especially when you want to get people to see things your way? Are you willing to try some new behavior? Do you know how to disagree tactfully or blatantly as the situation demands? Are you willing to take appropriate risks? Here's some important news: As an adult you have a choice about what you believe and what you discard. You do not need to hold yourself back, put yourself down, or become overly aggressive.

DIFFICULT PEOPLE LIKE IT THEIR WAY

Going a round or two with those who only want to see things their way might make you feel as if you've been run over by a tractor trailer or have gone through the spin cycle of your washing machine on high for about an hour. This is because many of you still believe that you have to tolerate it and that there is no better way to handle the situation. While you are trying to regain your composure, the person you were dealing with thinks that things turned out exactly as they should.

Bob told what had happened to him:

> I'd been working for this manager for about a year when I arrived late for our usual Wednesday morning production meeting. Everyone in the room was sitting around a table and I had to try to slip in to the back of the room so as not to disturb the discussion in progress. I really wanted a cup of coffee but I didn't want to call any extra attention to myself since the issue on the table was of a crucial nature. Just as I was settling in, the manager looked at me, put up his hand in a stopping gesture, and said in a very sarcastic voice, "Nice of you to join us, Bob, I hope we are not interfering in your day." At first I was horrified, and then as I thought of my child sick at home with a raging fever, I got really angry. But I kept my mouth shut because I knew that anything I could have said would have made it worse for me at that time.

If you were the person in this situation, you had a good reason for being late, and you were surrounded by others who felt the same way and supported you, what, if anything, would you have done differently? Difficult people such as this manager like the situation just as it is, and the people around them enable them and buy into it as well. To the manager, this was a regular day and there was nothing out of the ordinary. He prided himself on not being a pushover and believed that, if not for his strong leadership, no one would do any work. He also, in his own words, did not want to cut these people any slack because he was convinced that they would try to take advantage of his good nature. It didn't occur to him to approach Bob after the meeting to find out what was going on or to talk about how important it is to him to have everyone at the meeting. This was business as usual.

Single-minded people like this can have their cake and other people's too and will continue to do so as long as others buy into it, keep accepting it, and make allowances for how they behave.

A woman I know is married to a man with elderly parents and several children from a previous marriage. He is an executive with a large staff and plenty of money and time. So why is it that his wife attends to his parents? How does it happen that he invites people over and expects her to always entertain whom he wants, when he wants, and how he wants? Because *she does it*. She complains to her friends but says nothing to her husband. When I asked her why she doesn't say anything to him, she just sighed. "It's not worth getting him upset. That's just the way he is. He'll never change." Darn right he'll never change! Why should he? I wouldn't, in his position.

Tell me, if you had someone at home who took care of cooking, cleaning, and all your daily needs, or if you had people at the office who continually acquiesced to you (and all this while you got bigger raises, plum assignments, and more respect), would you want to upset the apple cart? Difficult people like it this way for a reason, and the reason is, it works for them.

Too often, it hasn't been necessary for difficult people to question their own behavior because others have kept silent about their feelings. Start by questioning yourself about your own propensity for attracting one or several varieties of the difficult-person species.

ARE YOU A DIFFICULT-PERSON MAGNET?

Now is a good time to begin the change process. Think about the people in your life. Some of them are wonderful, kind, considerate, and interesting—not necessarily easy but not destructive either. Not all of the people in your life are horrible. It's just that there are times when you feel angry or uncomfortable and out of control with some of them.

You may feel angry, frustrated, used, taken advantage of, talked down to, taken for granted, set up, let down, insulted, foolish, angry, or sad before, during, or after any contact with them. Not to say that these feelings are uncommon—they are not—and not to say that you can't feel these feelings with non-difficult individuals as well. You can. This is about the relentless, nagging, ungiving, confidence-eroding, and energy-draining stuff—the kind of behavior that makes you feel tired when you've just had a solid eight hours of sleep.

What's that? You're groaning, rolling your eyes, thinking about putting this book down and getting something to eat? Don't give up that easily. Difficult people who don't want to see it your way have to learn that, although they can be difficult somewhere else, the rules change when they're with you.

If you've ever wondered if you have "difficult-person radar" because they always seem to end up on your doorstep or in front of your desk at work, you need to find out exactly which specimens you attract. To do this, take the following quiz. Read each of the questions and check off the appropriate characteristics that difficult people in your work life exhibit and, lest you despair, hang on to the fact that you are not in this alone. There are others who are going through this with you.

Items 1 through 10 represent different composite descriptions of difficult people. Although it's true that all are different, it is possible to lump together some of their behaviors and come up with some main types, which you'll find in chapter 2. After you complete this quiz, you may find that you have checked off items spread throughout all ten sections or that your selections are clustered together in just one or two. Either way is fine. Your response pattern will indicate whether you're dealing with a "pure" difficult person or a "combo pack."

The "Are You a Difficult-Person Magnet?" Quiz

Think about the people you deal with at work and in your personal life.

1. Do they
   - Move in and take over?
   - Explode?
   - Push you around, verbally and emotionally?
   - Believe that might makes right (and, since they have might, of course they're right)?
2. Do they
   - Correct you in front of others?
   - Find fault with you and your ideas?
   - Blame you for everything?
   - Take responsibility for nothing?
3. Do they
   - See themselves as cool and logical?
   - Resent it when you become emotional?
   - Need to see proof of anything you say?
   - Reject ideas that they don't believe?

4. Do they
    - Pretend that they care and then make you feel stupid?
    - Keep you guessing and never really open up?
    - Tell you that you're doing a good job but won't let you do it your way?
    - Sucker you in and then drop you on your behind?
5. Do they
    - Take the best for themselves because they believe that they deserve it and you don't?
    - Take charge and tell you what to do?
    - Distance themselves and refuse to mingle with "just anyone"?
    - Take care of themselves at your expense?
6. Do they
    - Try to be the center of every situation?
    - Spread their hypothetical plumes when someone is watching?
    - Kick small dogs to make themselves look tough?
    - Believe that the size of their biceps or the size of their paychecks are directly proportional to the size of their brain?
7. Do they
    - Believe that they never have to justify their position?
    - Brag as if you should care?
    - Tell you they know it all, have seen it all, and have done it all?
    - Let you know how little you know?
8. Do they
    - Sweat when you say the "A" (accountability) word?
    - Give an immediate disclaimer about not being ready to meet a deadline?

- Always think that you're trying to trap them?
- Convince themselves that you're more concerned about the assignment or relationship than they are?

9. Do they
   - Always look as if they have been carrying the weight of the world on their shoulders?
   - "Nice" you to death?
   - Love being the fall guy?
   - Have one crisis after another?

10. Do they
    - Look for surrogate parents?
    - Refuse to grow up?
    - Still live at home, emotionally if not physically?
    - Act more like a child than an adult?

Hang on to your answers. As you proceed to chapter 2, you'll find out which people correspond to these groups, how they operate, and what you can do to change how you deal with them.

2

THE LINEUP

n this part of the process of dealing with people who don't want to see it your way, you get to stop, reflect, and take a very close look at them—closer than you usually have time to do when you are in a more reactive mode, working hard to keep your cool and possibly your sanity.

As you read the upcoming descriptions you will recognize many types of difficult behavior. You'll also notice that each type is a composite with some overlap from one to another, since these difficult individuals are a lot like chameleons—they change to blend into their environments.

Some of them are perfectly civil, fun, and easy to be with when alone with you, but put them in a room with others and they instantly exhibit a serious behavior metamorphosis. The most polite and genteel of them, when with a group of other people, will transform themselves into walking, talking trouble machines in about three seconds flat right before your very eyes. Are these difficult people born or made? It doesn't matter, as long as you're not the one contributing to their perpetuation.

The purpose of the upcoming lineup is to introduce you to the specific types of challenging persons and their behaviors. After the initial description of each, I present strategies for coping with them. The remaining chapters will detail the appropriate tools and techniques to employ these strategies.

To ensure that this examination is manageable, difficult persons who don't want to see it your way have been classified by ten types divided into three categories, based on what they most want or need from others. This classification system has been set up based on the quiz in chapter 1, so have your results ready.

The first category, the Powermongers, includes individuals who want power. In this category are the Destroyer (section 1 of the "Are You a Difficult-Person Magnet?" quiz), the Blamer (section 2), the Logic Pusher (section 3), and the Baiter-and-Switcher (section 4).

The second category, the Admiration Hounds, includes difficult individuals who want and need admiration from others. You may know the Executive (section 5), the Peacock (section 6), or the Self-Proclaimed Expert (section 7).

And, as if these aren't enough, stay tuned for our third and final category, comprising difficult people who want and need

THE LINEUP 23

TLC (tender, loving care) and nurturing: the Nurture Needers. You probably know the Accountability Phobic (section 8), the Victim (section 9), and the Spoiled Brat (section 10). If not, you're lucky, because they seem to be everywhere and multiplying at an alarming rate.

As you read about each of the three categories, instead of searching for the exact description of your antagonist, look for those symptoms that are most representative of him or her.

Keep in mind, there is no such thing as a "pure" type of difficult person. Your difficult and resistant person may be motivated by power but also might want some nurturing. He or she might be communicatively challenged when dealing with you but show no signs of this when with others. Or, the individual might be one way with you on Monday and somewhat different on Saturday. To deal with such complex behavior, you need an edge.

THE POWERMONGERS

Difficult persons motivated by power are not unlike the wolf in the children's story of the three pigs. Remember the line "I'll huff and I'll puff and I'll blow your house down"? Well, these people took it seriously and have made it a way of life. Their basic stance is that everyone involved in their lives, in any way, is meant to be conquered and controlled and that they're the ones to do it.

Can you reverse this dysfunctional pattern? No, but you can modify it. Difficult people who push for power need something to push against, and if you stop pushing, you take away the resistance they need to keep from falling on their face.

These are the main types of Powermongers: the Destroyer, the Blamer, the Logic Pusher, and the Baiter-and-Switcher. The following section discusses them one at a time.

The Destroyer

Description   Destroyers are those people who often like to play verbal kickball with you as the ball. These opponents can be loud and abrasive or quiet and seething. Their intense personalities often explode in anger and inappropriate behavior. At times, they might try to control everything you do by yelling and embarrassing you in front of others. They see only one way—their way—and they expect total compliance from you. They use intimidation on a regular basis, sometimes doing it with humor and other times with threats.

The woman Dave lived with would build him up with compliments in public, but in private she would tell him he was a mess. Her favorite control technique was the mind game. She'd say things like "You owe me for all I've done for you. You'll never go anywhere without me, and you'll never find another woman who will put up with you. If not for me, you'd have nothing."

Frank was the only nonfamily employee in a family business. He worked really hard and hoped that he would eventually advance to the point where he could buy into the business and become a shareholder. After years of Frank asking repeatedly and being strung along, the owner promoted his do-nothing son to executive vice president. When Frank confronted him, the owner told him that although Frank would never be a partner, he should be grateful to have a secure place to work. He made a point of telling Frank that he would never make it in another company because he didn't have the right personality.

Not all Destroyers are this intense and destructive. What they are is downright inconvenient to deal with. They have such a short fuse that they are totally unpredictable, or they flex their power by making it uncomfortable for you to refuse to do what they want.

Strategies   Many Destroyers are very enticing, but from the word go they deliberately set you up to be at their mercy. They intentionally try to control you, and you must be prepared either to reduce your resistance if the issue is not important or to be direct and assertive if you are unwilling to comply. These are the techniques you will find outlined in chapter 5, "Conflict Savvy." Also, you can sometimes use humor to defuse the situation, as long as the humor is not self-deprecating or aimed directly at the Destroyer.

Destroyers use strength and intensity to feel powerful. So when it makes sense—and only then—let them have their way: If you don't have a strong emotional investment (chapter 5), if you can live with it, and if you don't really care, don't go for the win. Avoid the issue. You can give the Destroyer feedback and try to negotiate, but make sure you are emotionally calm and cool enough to attempt this.

Pick low-risk issues to begin with. It is important to define the problem; adjust your attitude (chapter 3) by affirming your right to work on changing your situation; and choose your conflict position by deciding how important it is to you (chapter 5).

Sometimes, parting ways with a Destroyer is the only solution; at other times, you can either stand up to such a person or barter.

Many Destroyers also combine some qualities of the Executive, a member of the Admiration Hounds group. Their drive is motivated by their belief that they deserve everything and you deserve nothing. They have no qualms about what they do, and they have no respect or regard for you as a person.

Dee's boss told her to enter some figures into a report. When he reviewed her work, he thought that what she did was wrong, so he changed the numbers. A week later, her boss's manager called her in and said, "How could you be so stupid? Your numbers are wrong!" Dee went to her boss and said, "Why did you make me take the rap for your mistake?" to which he responded, "Because I'm going up in this company, and you're going nowhere, so it doesn't matter."

What did Dee do? She confronted and gave feedback (chapter 4). She told her boss that she was concerned that he had put a cap on her career development, and she wanted to work with him to develop a career plan. She also went to her boss's boss and told him that there must have been some confusion, because the numbers on the report did not match the numbers on her data sheets. She also offered him her data sheets. She didn't accuse her boss; she just excused herself.

The Blamer

Description   Because of their insecurity, Blamers have a strong emotional investment in saving face. It takes guts and self-esteem to be able to say, "I screwed up," or "Oops, that was no good," and Blamers don't want to take that risk. That's why they find the negatives in you. Pointing out what's not okay with you is their way of constantly trying to reaffirm what's okay about them. Champion guilt-givers, Blamers raise passive-aggressive behavior to new heights. Since nothing you do is ever right, they are convinced that nothing they ever do is wrong. These people can be very nasty, and you have to resist the tendency to snap back.

Take Christina, who wanted the coffee hot when clients came in to the office for meetings. Her assistant, Jackie, placed a cup of steaming coffee on the conference table in front of her. While Jackie was getting the cream and sugar from the lunch room down the hall, she heard Christina scream. When Jackie ran back into the conference room, Christina was livid, yelling,

"Don't you ever, I mean ever, place a cup of steaming hot coffee in front of me again!" She had burned her lip.

Here is a grown-up with no apparent disabilities wanting someone else to give her a food-temperature report and to take responsibility for her pouring it into her mouth without checking it first. A little self-righteous, perhaps?

Strategies   Most of your work with Blamers will consist of preparation activities. When you are dealing with Blamers who make you the scapegoat for all their errors and poor performance, you need to take notes while they talk and read the notes back to them before you make a move. Keep your special "note" journal in a highly visible spot on your desk so that the Blamers get used to seeing it. It will become a reminder that even though being accountable gives them cramps, they'd better get used to it. To make sure that you set the stage for putting the responsibility where it should go, ask a lot of open and closed questions (which you'll learn about in chapter 4) up front. This will help to eliminate any confusion and give you protection when the stuff starts hitting the fan.

If they say something critical like "You acted like a fool at dinner and if we lose the account, it's your fault," you can always answer, "Oh," or "Is that what you thought?" or "How would you have preferred I act?" or "When you want something specific from me, it would be helpful if you would let me know beforehand so that you and I might discuss it in as much detail as necessary."

If you choose to confront Blamers when they are being critical, when they say, "You would say something like that," use a clarifying question (chapter 4). Answer, "That sounded like a dig. Is that what you intended?" Then deal with whatever answer you get. If they say yes, you say, "There's nothing I can do to respond to a dig. If you tell me specifically what you are referring to, I am willing to discuss it with you."

Their belief is that they are too important to take responsibility for anything. That's why they blame you. Don't try to knock down their belief. When they begin to criticize, imagine that they're putting mud on a silver tray and handing it to you. Look at the mud on the tray and say to yourself, "Hmmm, mud on a sterling silver tray. It's a nice silver tray. Still, I don't want mud, I don't need mud, and I'm not going to pick mud up." When Blamers do their thing, instead of getting suckered into a battle, remain neutral. This takes practice, yet it can be done. If they criticize or judge you, so be it. In your mind, think, "Okay, I heard that. Now what?" Wait for them to speak again. Don't get defensive. Instead, get pensive. Watch, wait, and listen. Dealing effectively with the Blamer, then, means positioning yourself so that you maintain self-control; it means being able to ask open and closed questions that will enable you to uncover information (proof) afterward. It also means being able to confront without being defensive, hostile, or emotional. These are all the skills you will hone in chapter 4.

The Logic Pusher

Description   The Logic Pushers are the people who get annoyed when, according to them, you try to clutter facts with feelings. They are truly inconvenienced by emotions and find dealing with them messy, impossible, and irritating. They make their case with data and that's all they care about, and they use their facts as weapons, a way to control you. They might be Technoids or Number Nerds, and they've never met an authority or a statistic they didn't like. If you can't prove it to them, it just doesn't exist.

It is not uncommon to have a department of individuals, who, when reporting to a Logic Pusher, all complain that they never get any positive feedback. The Logic Pusher, when told this, always says the same thing: "They still have their jobs, don't they? Isn't that enough of a positive message? What else do they want from me?"

Logic Pushers can be cold or they can be neutral (which is not quite as icy as cold, but not warm and inviting either). Their worlds are black-and-white, all-or-nothing, yes or no. They have no patience for opinions or feelings, only for facts that can be substantiated. They believe their own facts much more than they believe yours, and they expect that anybody who is an emotional being will probably be short on facts and long on irrational feelings and opinions. They can be shrewd and cunning, always looking for an angle, a way to justify their own beliefs.

Strategies Whenever someone disagrees with Shel, he makes his case, and then machine-guns that person with questions. When I first met him, I was slightly taken back because I really felt like I was on a hot seat and had to defend myself. Then I got smart.

I decided to try a new approach, pulling Shel off course. You have to know Shel to really appreciate this; he is a person who is meticulous about everything, including his appearance, so this was the soft underbelly I decided to prod. In the middle of one of his inquisitions, I suddenly looked him up and down and said, "Excuse me, Shel, I hate to ask you this, but have you put on a few pounds? Your cheeks look really different now, they look like chipmunk cheeks." I couldn't have chosen better. After Shel denied it vehemently, reviewing his eating and exercise schedule with me in great detail, I looked at him in my most understanding way and said, "Of course, you haven't gained weight. I probably need new glasses. Now, what were you asking me?" To Shel's credit, and because he has a great sense of humor, he got it! He paused, looked me in the eye, and chuckled. "Point taken," he said.

It's all about using humor, in addition to skill. All I did was ask a question, and it completely changed the dynamics of the situation. By the way, Shel and I have become good friends, and we still tease each other. When dealing with a Logic Pusher and humor isn't the answer, you must do two things. First, control your emotions. Put them aside, and save them for people who care. You can have them, just don't expect them to be acknowledged. Second, do your homework. If they listen to logic, give them logic. Don't make emotional appeals. They are meaningless and will ultimately work against you in that the Logic Pusher will discount you for having them in the first place. The more proof you can offer, the better. Anything in writing (documentation) would be helpful. Instead of saying, "This is how I feel about . . ." say, "This is what makes this situation important" and use words like *implications* and *impact*. You can't "out-logic" a Logic Pusher. If they really start chugging along, just step aside and let them run their course. Don't be intimidated and don't compromise your beliefs. Do ask questions that will give you the opportunity to poke holes in their pitch.

Let a Logic Pusher talk, and if you're so inclined, respond with, "The information you gave me is very interesting. It's hard to grasp so much at once. Where can I read more about it on my own?" Make sure that you don't sound sarcastic when you say this.

Use visuals when you talk to them; body language is very important. For example, say, "I have three points to make regarding this issue," and then hold up three fingers and count off the issues as you bring them up.

Marta went to a conference where she was one of two women with seven men in a problem-solving simulation group. One of the men immediately took over, barking orders, and began making decisions based on financial information that the group had to work with. Whenever Marta made suggestions, he dismissed her and pointed back to the figures on the page.

Marta chose the right time and place (which we will discuss in chapter 5) and said, "Up until now, during our discussions about strategy, you dismissed what I said, interrupted me, and didn't really listen to my input. Here are some examples of what I'm talking about." After she cited the examples, she then proceeded to tell him how she wanted and had a right to be treated. She held her own, kept her focus on his behavior and what she had a right to in this situation, didn't sink to making personal attacks or insults, maintained direct eye contact, and finally wore him down. Marta refers to the situation as one in which she "tamed a bronco." She and her Logic Pusher actually developed a good working relationship over the next nine days.

When dealing with Logic Pushers, don't throw the baby out with the bathwater! Use them when you need research material or advice. If they are Technoids, when you need computer advice, it might be worth putting up with their lectures to get the information you need. Another bonus is that they will want to follow through on whatever they say they will do for you because they want to look good. Take advantage of it. Ask them questions that they can relate to and answer easily, and let them feel good about themselves and their knowledge. The following questions are two that are particularly useful:

"What do you see as the implications?"

"What would be the logical next step?"

After you've read the section on questions in chapter 4, prepare yourself immediately by making a list that you can use with Logic Pushers. It never hurts to get ready in advance.

When dealing with Logic Pushers, keep your cool and detach yourself emotionally. Visualize the Logic Pusher as a big computer with a head (sporting a bad haircut, perhaps), weird glasses, and flat feet with tennis shoes. This will help you keep your perspective. Logic Pushers often come across as very cold and uncaring, and your job is to stop expecting them to care so that you won't constantly be disappointed.

This is a difficult individual who requires that you be ready with facts or moves. Questioning and feedback skills will serve you well here, as will knowing when to speak up and when to clam up (chapter 5).

The Baiter-and-Switcher

Description   Baiters-and-Switchers are the difficult people who use your feelings as a weapon against you. They pull you toward them in one emotionally seductive way or another, and the minute you surrender, they'll push you away. They maneuver so that you do all the work, and they take all the credit. They look like caring people, they sound like caring people, but they're not. They're frauds. They are noncommunicators about real issues, and the game they play is "Guess What I'm Thinking; Wrong, Guess Again." They're good at turning you on, then tuning you out.

That's how they control you, by constantly changing the game and the rules—and what skill they display doing it! They are smooth. When they ask you how you feel, they do it in such a way that you really believe they want to know, and they know just how to phrase their questions and just how to look at you.

That's why it's so chilling when, after you have let down your guard, they immediately switch off, dismiss you, and focus on something totally different.

Most Baiters-and-Switchers are really good at removing your barriers, and at those infrequent times when they do encounter resistance, they have two or three stockpiled, soft-touch, sensitivity stories they pull out and use to soften you up. And when you take the bait, they quickly change the tone of their dealings with you and put their stories away for the next time they want to penetrate your armor. Their trick is to make you feel comfortable; lull you into a false sense of security, trust, and acceptance; and then slam the door shut. You're trapped.

Dorothy's boss started the day by asking her why she seemed a little down. When Dorothy answered that it wasn't important enough to discuss (which, by the way, is another self-deprecating thing that some people do to erode their own importance and credibility), her boss pushed her to open up. When Dorothy began to reveal her true feelings concerning something that had upset her the previous week, the boss responded, "I can't believe you're making such a big deal about this." Dorothy felt embarrassed about having shown her true feelings, and she vowed never to open up again. But, of course, unless she changes the dynamics of her relationship with the Baiter-and-Switcher, she will open up again and get kicked in the stomach many more times.

Tony encountered a slightly different Baiter-and-Switcher. One day his boss came over to him and asked if everything was okay, because Tony didn't look like his usual self. When Tony told him that he was worried about his sick daughter, his boss told him to take the rest of the day off to take care of her. Two weeks later, his boss gave an important project that Tony was supposed to get to one of his coworkers. When Tony asked why, the boss complained that he couldn't count on Tony to be reliable; Tony didn't have his priorities straight.

Strategies   So what can you do with a difficult person like this? Simple. Don't take the bait. If you do take the bait, as soon as you realize it, resolve not to take the bait again—ever! Don't walk around with the word sucker on your forehead. Everyone can make a mistake once, but twice, forget it! Your biggest mistake will be to see this duplicitous person as having potential as a human being because you've experienced his or her "soft" side. The Baiter-and-Switcher has no soft, feeling, or sensitive side, only a slimy underbelly. So don't confuse the two.

When people waste their lives and careers on people like this, it destroys their self-esteem in the process. Don't get lured into the "maybe they'll change" web. Such people are dangerous. They want to tug at your strings and watch you jump and dance around. They want to control you as they would a puppet. Don't let them get to your guts. They only want to sprinkle salt on them.

Joe knew that Matt really wanted to have a chance to present a new concept to a client. Joe told Matt that if he did all the work and put together the entire presentation, he would be the one to present. The day finally came. Just before they went into the conference room, Joe asked Matt how he was feeling. Matt said that he was really nervous, and Joe told him to relax because there was nothing to be nervous about. When everyone was seated and Matt opened his mouth to speak, Joe stood up and began the presentation. He didn't sit down and proceeded to deliver the entire presentation by himself, leaving Matt speechless in more ways than one. After the meeting, when Joe and Matt were walking to the parking garage, Matt looked at Joe and said that he thought that if he was to do the work, he was also to do the presentation. Joe responded by telling Matt that he took over because Matt had said that he was nervous and that he couldn't risk the contract just because Matt wanted to try something new.

Baiters-and-Switchers are more than just difficult, they are downright dishonest, and there is no valid excuse for being that way. Baiters-and-Switchers also have other characteristics that make them doubly troubling. You may sometimes encounter a Baiter-and-Switcher who is on the cusp of the Blamer, so be prepared. Claire still remembers a time when George said to her, "You never want to share your feelings with me. You never tell me what's going on with you. You get jumpy. You treat me badly and I don't know why."

George then plopped himself down on the couch with an expression that reminded Claire of a depressed basset hound. As soon as Claire started to explain her frustration, George began telling her that he was never to blame and that Claire was the one screwing up the relationship.

Claire now knows that when she loses her temper, it is nonproductive and makes things worse, and that it is much better when she asks open questions (chapter 4) to find out what's upsetting George. If either of them gets too upset, she leaves the room, saying that she will come back and discuss it later.

This is a good tactic to use because it keeps you in control or helps you regain it quickly if you've lost it. You'll learn more about this kind of positioning in chapter 5.

Be very careful when you deal with Baiters-and-Switchers. Keep them at arm's length. No matter how charming and friendly they try to get, draw a definite line in the relationship. It is too easy to start talking and opening up to them as you would a close friend, only to find that if you talk, you will pay, and pay, and pay. Guard yourself against being taken in by the Baiters-and-Switchers of the world. Be suspicious of people who are "overcomplimentary," especially in front of other people.

If your difficult person is a Baiter-and-Switcher, as you read on, pay particular attention to the section on how to adjust your attitude (chapter 3). Decide whether it is worth it to you to speak up or clam up (chapter 5). If speaking up is your choice, don't talk feelings, because to these difficult individuals feelings mean vulnerability, and they salivate at the thought of getting their hooks into you. Talk about behavior, interpretations, and results. Cut your emotional investment; cancel it, in fact, since these difficult individuals are going nowhere in the feeling department. Choose a confrontation technique (chapter 4) that you feel comfortable with and stick to it. Study, practice, and learn to use open questions to get them to tell you more about their agenda. You may want to throw in a little guilt (chapter 5); it can't hurt.

THE ADMIRATION HOUNDS

Difficult people motivated by admiration include the Executive, the Peacock, and the Self-Proclaimed Expert. These presidents of their own fan clubs have the basic attitude that they are really hot and that you are not, and they want you to agree with this assessment, loudly, openly, and often. Their basic stance is that others are put on this earth to make them look good. They expect no competition from you, and they want you to defer to them in the attention department.

The Executive

Description Executives are often empire-builders who want you as a subject. At work, they take the best assignments and give you the dregs. You are supposed to put their wants and needs first. Their belief is that they're too important to do the work; they expect you to do it for them. They're convinced that they deserve the best and that you are there to give it to them.

Bill's boss, Susan, made a mistake with a customer. She told Bill to write a letter of apology to the customer and to sign his own name. Susan explained that it would look bad for the company if someone at Susan's level were wrong, but that no one would be surprised if someone at Bill's level were. Ridiculous as these people are in the self-inflated ego department, they are also dangerous because of their condescending behavior. And if there's one thing that wastes your time and energy, it's condescending, difficult people.

A lot of Executives started from nothing and built their new images to their own exact specifications. Many think they are above everything and everybody else. They want to be seen as having been born with the proverbial silver spoon in their mouths. They want people to revere them, and if you—as a coworker, subordinate, or service provider—are not interested in revering them, they will work on insisting that you come around to their way of thinking.

When confronted with something they've done, they refuse to acknowledge that the problem is with them. They need to have someone obey them in order to feel important. They want to be put on a pedestal, admired, and respected. They really think that they are above everybody else. They expect you to handle all the details, clean up after them, and make them look as impressive as they really think they are. Often, when Executives meet you, they love who you are. They say, "You're outgoing, you're assertive, and you're sharp. You seem highly motivated, and you're smart." Then, after a short time, they start to criticize the same qualities for which they admired you in the beginning, because they're afraid that someone else (another person, another company) will want you, that you'll leave them, and that they'll look bad.

Strategies Since Executives want attention, give them attention. If they have big egos, feed their egos, get it over with, watch them calm down, and move on. You have to clarify your intent with Executives. If it's to knock them down a peg or two, you're on the wrong track. Your job is to concentrate on maintaining control of yourself, not them. If they give you the bum part of a job at work, talk about requiring continuity to complete the task so that it comes out of their department up to their usual high standards. Talk about them as your coach and mentor and express how much their senior savvy helps you do things well.

Such people exercise control by keeping you in a deferential position. If up until now you have been resisting, confuse them by treating them like executives so that you can maneuver and get what you want.

These are the type of people to barter with. Offer to do something extra for them, something you know that they want (it can't be illegal, immoral, unethical, sexual, or fattening) and put in a proviso for you. Be direct with Executives if you think they are trying to use you or make you look bad. Use one of the confrontation techniques to be discussed (chapter 4): describe what you see or hear; give them your interpretation and ask for an explanation; then close your mouth, tightly, and don't get hooked into filling silent space.

At all times, clearly define your boundaries. "I know you don't like to do the proofreading. It is a waste of your time. That's why I thought you'd enjoy concept development. It requires much more skill." Or "I know that you don't like to take the kids shopping for their school clothes but you are so much better at helping them choose affordable things that look good without going for the expensive stuff that all their friends want."

Abby's boss, Jim, sees himself as an open, fair, easy-to-approach, nonsexist, nonjudgmental person. In fact, he is the exact opposite. He is very stubborn, and when he makes up his mind about an issue, there is very little she can do to get him to look at another side of it. He has been known to say that "a woman couldn't handle this type of job." Although he says that he is approachable, when she acts friendly he withdraws into his pompous mode. His body language changes and lets her know she hasn't been deferential enough.

Abby deals with Jim by being personable, not personal. She has learned always to show that she knows that he is important, and, in return, he does favors for her and engages her as a confidante. If you want to get things from Executives, praise them and reinforce what they do and say. Don't be critical of them, because they see no middle ground. To them, you're either with them or against them, so watch yourself. Executives can be vindictive, because they are very competitive. They have no intention of sacrificing their status for you or your needs. You are expendable if you don't add to their aura. Make them feel good about themselves and work your agenda around them.

The Peacock

Description Peacocks shuffle people like a deck of cards, always trying to get a better hand. When it comes to their image, they spend more time on themselves than anybody else. They never pass a mirror or a plate-glass window without giving themselves an admiring glance.

Peacocks can be difficult people to deal with. They think they are terrific and want you to think so, too. They are arrogant, self-centered, self-consumed, and usually very, very boring to be around. There's only one way to do things—their way—and they think that you should be grateful to have the opportunity to do anything related to them. They want to be the center of attention and are part of that rare breed of people who actually like to work a room. Initially, they appear to be great at company mixers, meetings, conventions, parties, and any event that involves social interaction. They sometimes make a good first impression because of the ease with which they start conversations with others. Since overused or inappropriately used strengths often become weaknesses, Peacocks tends to do too much of a good thing. They are so concerned about getting to talk to everybody that when they are talking to you, you often notice them looking around the room for their next hobnobber. In their minds, they believe that anyone should be flattered to get the chance to be with them. They are exhausting to deal with. The wrapping may actually be great, but the gift inside is usually a disappointment. The Peacock can have a large smattering of Executive mixed in.

Strategies   How do you deal with Peacocks? Never expect honesty from these difficult people; they delude themselves and believe their own delusions, and since they aren't forthright with themselves, how can they ever be with you?

Peacocks make themselves vulnerable because they are so dependent on you to feel vibrant. If you want your way with Peacocks, feed their egos, give them positive reinforcement, then strike when the iron is hot. If they want to prove their uniqueness, let them. People who want to prove that they are strong by single-handedly carrying your furniture down the hall to your new home office should have your blessing. If you want to take a Peacock to a boring dinner so that they will do all the talking and all you have to do is try to keep your eyes open while you are thinking about being somewhere else, go for it.

For those times when Peacocks are in particularly good form and you want a comeback and have nothing to lose, you might enjoy a couple of the phrases found in chapter 6. Male Peacocks become really obnoxious when they are womanizers. Female Peacocks become equally so when they are inappropriately seductive. Either type of behavior is very unattractive, and you can choose if and when to do something about it. Choose your battles carefully, using the different "conflict routes" coming up in chapter 5, and keep them off balance by using questions that are probing (chapter 4).

The Self-Proclaimed Expert

Description Self-Proclaimed Experts think they are just that, experts. They have an opinion on everything. They are the human answer to the hot-air balloon. They're the best, the greatest, and the brightest. No matter what you've accomplished, they've done more. They know it all, and you know nothing. They brag about everything they've done in life, from kindergarten on. They're legends in their own minds. They're always right. They dominate every conversation and relate everything you say back to themselves. They probably wouldn't mind a bit if you bowed slightly when they entered a room. They like to think on your feet instead of on theirs. They won't hesitate to tell you the right way to do something. They're beyond reproach.

Ethan works with a woman named Carol, who has an answer for everything. No matter what the subject of conversation, she is the supreme source of knowledge. If you are talking about law, she speaks with so much conviction that someone who didn't know her would think she had a law degree. If you're talking about medicine, she has all the answers and knows exactly what course of treatment you should follow. If you disagree with her, she is incensed. How dare you question her omniscience!

Self-Proclaimed Experts never see flaws when they look in the mirror. They see wisdom, knowledge, experience, and probably holiness. That's why they can't imagine any person not feeling grateful for any shred of knowledge that they are willing to impart. While Peacocks see themselves as the acme of physical perfection, Self-Proclaimed Experts consider themselves the height of mental prowess.

You know the type: big shots, know-it-alls, and experts on everything. They puff up and strut around like they're really hot stuff; or they sit back and are right all the time, and control by being wise. Because they want to be recognized for being the best and the brightest, they have a need to be superpowers, which means that they want you to defer to them. They want admiration, use intimidation, and like to be in charge of everything so that they can get the credit for it; and, of course, they take credit even when it's not theirs to take. They're condescending, patronizing, and frustrating to deal with. The phrase "I don't know" is one they've never mouthed.

Strategies   Let Self-Proclaimed Experts take charge if you must, but don't make it too easy for them. Pay attention to what they say; then try to follow their orders and get them to help you because they are so smart and so competent. While Executives want to be served, keep in mind that Self-Proclaimed Experts have egos that need to be fed or they become cranky and annoying. Ask them to coach you, to guide you, and to share their wisdom with you. Tell them that they are an interesting and important role model. They don't have to know that they're the one role model you never want to emulate.

Listen to and acknowledge what they say, but don't confront them directly. Challenging them will only make things worse. Ask a lot of clarifying questions, combining open and closed (chapter 4). Get them to do the work for you or at least to plan it out. Pick their brains for as many ideas as you can. If you do need to disagree, make sure you do it with solid information. If they are convinced that their way is better, and they are resisting yours, say something like, "I'm excited about working hard to enhance your ideas," or "People will go crazy with joy when they see the next level you'll have taken this to."

Again, your goal is to deal with them and get what you want or to get them to see it your way, not to change them. Always keep that in mind. Don't lose your focus.

You can cash in on Self-Proclaimed Experts' need to be admired not only by getting them to do a lot of your work but by getting them to take overall responsibility for projects. If they like the limelight, give it to them when you know that it would be highly risky for you to take it without their support.

If they do help you out, don't be too grateful. Acknowledge their actions and move on.

If you let Self-Proclaimed Experts know that you don't admire them, they'll probably go away. If that's what you want, great. But if you need them, remember to feed their all-knowing egos. If you don't fawn over them, or if you tell them straight that you don't like what they do or that you don't respect them as informed individuals, they will usually cut off the relationship, because they can't stand it when they're not treated like sages. So be careful. Don't cut them loose just because they tick you off.

If you have an investment in the relationship (for example, if it's with your boss or in-law), you can protect yourself with praise, and the thicker you pour it on, the better. Ask them to share their knowledge and expertise with you. Ask for their advice. Request that they give you the benefit of their vast experience and let you run some ideas by them for their input. At work, Self-Proclaimed Experts base their decisions about how to deal with you and how generous to be on how much they think you like them. If they think you like them a lot, they'll do anything for you. Don't worry about being right or being deserving in order to get what you want. They see themselves as fountains of information; turn on their spigots and let them spew.

You can use them to do things you don't want to do, or you can keep them dangling by varying the amount of reverence you give them. If you want to get really good at doling it out, check the section on "Politically Correct Confronting" in chapter 4. You'll get a lot of good ideas about how to pile it on with style.

THE NURTURE NEEDERS

Accountability Phobics, Victims, and Spoiled Brats are difficult individuals motivated by the need to be nurtured or taken care of. They are similar to those who need admiration and are easier to deal with than those motivated by the need for power. Their basic stance is that they are helpless victims who need you to acknowledge how difficult life is for them and how much they suffer. They want others to recognize the sacrifices they make and to understand that they are fragile and sensitive. They don't want to be hurt; they want to be protected and insulated; and they certainly don't want to be challenged. These are the people who want to show up in life and have someone else lead them through it. And if that someone is you, then at work and in life, you are doing two jobs and getting paid for one.

The Accountability Phobic

Description Accountability Phobics are black holes of emotional need. These difficult individuals don't want to have to give. They want to take, and they control you by needing more and more from you without ever giving anything back. Brad approached the facilitator at the end of a management training class and asked for help in dealing with his boss of six years, a true Accountability Phobic. "He tells me that he is going to give me some major accounts to work on so that I can get some experience and visibility and begin moving toward a more senior position. He promises that he will coach me, and when I ask him when this arrangement will begin, he says, 'Don't pressure me. Trust me. When the time is right I'll let you do it.'"

Now, if Brad asked you for advice, what would you tell him? Probably that his boss will not be accountable for his commitment. Forget it and move on. He'll only continue to string you along. Accountability Phobics are experts at this, and it can be exhausting to deal with them. They won't be pinned down. You want a delivery date or the date of completion of a project? Getting one is like pulling teeth, and then they still don't follow through. Some Accountability Phobics are perfectionists, and their behavior is a way of saying that nothing will ever be right enough, so why even try? It is a convenient curtain to hide behind.

Accountability Phobics can drive you crazy with their inde-cisiveness. Not to say that they aren't also charming, because they are, and this is what makes them even more frustrating. They appear to get so close to action, and then—whooooosh! They're gone. Avoidance is their middle name. Those who have a strong need to help other people are the best targets of these individuals.

Strategies   How do you deal with Accountability Phobics? Very slowly and deliberately, to be sure. You have to contract with them up front for small things, since they are totally over-whelmed by anything big. They are so controlling when they begin to back away that you have to guard against letting them suck the life out of you.

Don't try to bring about any kind of rapid or even average change with these people, because change makes them nervous. They like things the way they are because they feel more in control that way.

Rose had a chance to test her conflict savvy (chapter 5) and her problem-solving abilities when she went out on a blind date with a man who seemed very interesting and fun. She didn't make any assumptions, however, and decided to let him take the lead. At first she was horrified, and then she was amused, that on their second date, while having coffee, he looked at her with utmost seriousness and said, "I don't want to hurt you. I know that you are really going to fall for me, but I've just come off of a bad relationship experience, and I won't be able to give you what you want. I can't give you all of me, and I know you'll be devastated. I want to keep seeing you, but I don't want you ever to expect me to settle down or have a really serious relationship. I've been badly burned, and it has ruined me for other women."

Rose didn't know whether to laugh, applaud, or leave. What would you have done? She stayed and she played it cool. She didn't have to play hard to get because she *was* hard to get. Had he asked her, he would have found out that she wasn't humming "Here Comes the Bride" when he rang her doorbell. She had no expectations that this would turn into anything, so it really didn't matter. Emotionally, she had no feelings of ownership. (By the way, after a few years, they actually did get married and have remained so; and by the end, it was his idea. You just never know.)

Some Accountability Phobics are salvageable, but usually only when being unaccountable is not worth it for them.

What else do you do with Accountability Phobics? Find out what is at the root of their unwillingness to take responsibility. Is it based on fact, feeling, past experience, or what? Make it easy for them to tell you the truth. Learn to ask questions without a heavy dose of emotionalism, empathy, or guilt. For example: "If you did commit to a completion date for this project, what problems do you think might arise that would make meeting the deadline difficult for you?" You can also ask them a very direct, closed question, "What will it take for you to be accountable?" and when they answer, follow up with open questions to learn more about what they are basing their answers on.

Another method for dealing with Accountability Phobics is to use questions that give them forced choices, such as "Are you willing to just attend the meeting or do a presentation at the meeting?" This is also a good time to use the problem-solving model coming up in chapter 4; you can learn more about the barriers they are putting up in their mind and how to take them down, one at a time.

Give Accountability Phobics a lot of positive reinforcement when they make even the smallest commitment and keep it.

Don't gush so much that they have to dig themselves out from under, but do be direct and complimentary in specific terms: "You said you'd do the graphics for this presentation for me by today, and you did. It means a lot to me and to the client. Thank you."

Use what you will learn about body language in chapter 4 when dealing with Accountability Phobics, and establish direct eye contact. Don't stare or glare, but don't avert your eyes either. Use a moderate tone of voice; don't whine or demand, and make no assumptions. Since Accountability Phobics want to be taken care of, they also respond well to a lot of the emotions wasted on the Powermonger or Admiration Hound. It is often helpful to tell them how you feel as a result of their behavior. Don't use guilt if you can help it, because they're likely to bolt from the pressure.

The Victim

Description   Victims are the ostriches of the lineup. Since they like to keep their heads in the sand, their rear ends are exposed and up in the air a lot: a clear invitation to kick them around.

The fact that they prefer to hide in a bucket of sand, though, doesn't mean you should provide one for them. These people are big chickens. The thought of making a tough decision gives them cramps. They crumble under pressure and are often known to whine and squirm. They do a stellar imitation of a doormat.

Victims can be slugs as well, the type of difficult people who sit around so much that after a while you are convinced they have grown roots. As slugs, they have no energy or desire to think, say, or do anything. The world happens without them, and that's just the way they like it. They're good at getting other people to do things for them so that they don't have to do anything for themselves. They're different from the Executive, however, because they feel and communicate that they are not worthy. They want to feel safe and secure, a condition they perpetuate by resisting most changes. They deny having strong feelings because they don't want to have to do anything about them. They want people to accept them.

When forced to do anything, they become skilled procrastinators, their theory being that if they wait long enough, whatever you wanted them to do will no longer be necessary or important. This ploy often works, since many people just give up and do it themselves.

Victims want to be pampered, nurtured, and taken care of, not unlike a child; and if they can't be, they want to be left alone. When children need an out, they often cop out by saying, "My mother says I can't," even if they haven't asked her. It is a safe way to set and keep limits. Keep this behavior in mind when you are dealing with Victims because, like children, they don't have the courage to flat-out say, "I don't want to." Instead, they worm, weasel, stall, and zone out—anything to change the channel so you'll stop pressuring them.

How does one recognize Victims? They're never the bad guys. Somebody else is always to blame. They say things to those they supervise like, "I hate to do this. I don't agree with it, but *my* boss says we have to." They automatically assume a victim stance.

John, an accountant, is afraid to tell clients the job will cost more than was originally discussed. He waits until the end, and then surprises the client. He says, "You owe us another $100,000." When the client gets upset, he becomes even more victimized and retreats even further. The client gets angry; John feels like a loser and decides that he can't win. He gives himself permission to stop trying, and someone else has to bail him out.

Strategies   There is not that much you can do with these difficult people who have an investment in not seeing things your way. You can engage them, bypass them, or manipulate them. You do have to watch that they don't set you up by "yess-ing" you and building false expectations about that which they will or will not deliver. And at work, don't expect them to go to bat for you.

If your boss is a Victim, and you want him to ask his boss to approve a raise for you, don't hold your breath. The only chance you have is if you coach him through it and somehow convince him that doing this for you would be the lesser of two evils. Victims look for outlets for the frustration they don't usually allow themselves to release. They sometimes act irrationally just to release steam. Decide when to speak up and when to clam up (chapter 5). Be prepared to clean up any mess they make if their action involves you, because they'll retreat soon after they've acted out. Pay attention to who their advice-givers are and try to be one of them. If you can't make the inner circle, at least try to influence those who do. Don't waste your time on Victims, unless you know you can control their behavior.

Keep this in mind: once a Victim, almost always a Victim. Victims can be an extension of you; if you are a powerful person, they will piggyback on your success and blame you for any fail-ures. Resist the urge to take care of them. You can be helpful, but only if you set clear limits, and always try to get to the Victim first and last so that the other people trying to influence them in between won't be able to.

Strong people often won't bother with Victims. They just work around or go over them. This intimidates the Victims, and they become even more the Victim, or they agree to do things and then never get them done.

People find themselves in personal or professional relationships with Victims for different reasons. Sometimes it's because they themselves have no self-confidence. Sometimes it's just because they want to be with an easygoing, noncombative person, not realizing that "noncombative" really spells "jellyfish." And sometimes it's because they are very strong and they want to be with someone they can control.

When insecure people develop self-confidence or when strong people get tired of getting nothing in return, they may decide that it's time to redefine their relationships with Victims so that they don't run the risk of being bored.

Victims don't stand up for themselves, and this can be frustrating. The best way to deal with them is not to challenge them but to build a nonthreatening relationship in which they don't have to compete.

Victims need to feel connected to you. Victims like to bond and make personal contact. Even if they are analytical types who do nothing more than stay behind closed office doors playing with their computers or timid homebodies who sit on their couches watching television because they are hiding from the world, be as personable as you can to make them feel more secure. Ask for their ideas and their input. Make them feel special. Build them up now so that you can make requests of them later. This is a gradual process, so don't pile it on all at once. Pace yourself. Try a compliment or acknowledgment of something they've done and watch their reaction. Ask questions (chapter 4), even questions as simple as: "The purple cover is great! What made you decide to try a purple cover on your report this time?"

Ask them to do small things, and give them as much time as possible to do them. Check in with them regularly, and give them permission to have problems. Say things like "Nothing ever goes totally smoothly for anyone." Give them an easy question to answer: "What are some of the things that are going well?" Then add a more focused question: "What are some of the things not going so well?" You will be encouraging them to tell you by giving them permission to say anything at all. Some people are the "get right to the point" type. Victims are not. They need to talk over lunch or coffee. They need to be pumped up and stroked. Talk about the kind of work relationship they'd like with you and express your enthusiasm about getting to know them better. Remember that an ostrich takes its head out of the sand only if it is sure there isn't someone with an axe looking over its shoulder. To them, life just isn't fair, and there is always something wrong. Don't add to their grief; be the sun shining through their dark clouds.

A lot of people look like Victims on the outside but are really passive-aggressive on the inside. They'll sit back and not say anything, listen and take it all in, and then use the information they've gleaned in negative, underhanded ways. Watch for hidden agendas with people who are seemingly Victims. They could be closet Blamers, and if they are, go back and reread the prescription section for Blamers.

If Victims are the difficult people who don't want to see it your way, pay particular attention to the feedback, questioning, and timing techniques in the next two chapters.

The Spoiled Brat

Description   Now we come to Spoiled Brats, the difficult people, who, like Peter Pan, won't grow up. Behaving as an adult would mean having to accept responsibility and own up to their own wants, needs, feelings, and opinions. What they really want is for you to take care of them, stop making demands, and even wipe their noses (figuratively speaking). They expect you to run interference for them, keep them safe, and do those things that will please them.

Even though they may be in their twenties, forties, or sixties, they have never really grown up. These are people who want their way, and they want to find people and places where they can get their way without having to do anything they don't want to do. When they don't get their way, they throw temper tantrums and become moody, belligerent, or disengaged. It is not a pretty sight. It is not unusual for Spoiled Brats to manipulate the situations in which they find themselves. What are some of the danger signs?

1. They start sentences with "Why do I have to be the one to do this? Why can't you ask someone else?"
2. They don't seem to get it, and laugh at inappropriate times. You are trying to be serious about getting them to listen and participate and they seem to be on another planet.
3. They are not aware of the feelings of others. In fact, it never occurs to them that anybody else has feelings.
4. Since they have always done what they wanted to, they have little or no self-discipline.

The bad news is that, on the one hand, Spoiled Brats may be very nice people who will be attracted to you because you remind them of someone who has permitted them to take over and get their own way. On the other hand, they may be repelled by you for the very same reason. They may very well have a passive-aggressive streak. They may have a lot of unresolved issues with permissive people and have difficulty with strong and dominating individuals. They may do some Baiter-and-Switcher maneuvers, like opening

up the communication channel just a bit and then switching sta-
tions when you say something they don't want to hear.

Strategies When dealing with Spoiled Brats, be very aware of
the fact that these people will do and see things your way only if
the way you want something matches what they want as well.
You need to make these challenging people see that what they
have to offer has to be focused and directed. You have to work
on making it possible for them to build their self-esteem based
on their accomplishments. These people need all the redirection
that they can get and you can give them if they are ever going to
see it your way. You also have to set some boundaries. If you are
involved with Spoiled Brats, take special note of the confrontation and feedback tools coming up in chapter 4 and the
responses to put-downs you'll find in chapter 6.

So now you've seen them, in all their glory, the different
types of difficult people who don't want to see it your way. Some
are dangerous; others can be fun to deal with because their
behavior is actually quite ridiculous. They are all challenging,
however, especially when they are in power positions or are trying to control you.

The next step is to learn about how your attitudes may be
holding you back from dealing effectively with these difficult people. It can be easy for you to adjust your attitude and begin to
turn these difficult relationships around. You can make your communication better, articulate your ideas, and get what you want.

3

THE PARTY

IS OVER

ealing with people, and espe-
cially those who don't want to
see it your way, is a matter of
trial and error (mostly error).
Think of yourself as being on a journey
that has endless possibilities. You know
that you are an effective person in most
areas of your life, maybe not in the perfect or stellar range all the time, but at
least effective enough to have achieved
significant results. You know that you
don't intentionally try to get difficult
people to take advantage of you or treat

you shabbily. Perhaps in the past some people have treated you as a second-class citizen, and perhaps, unknowingly, you have reinforced the very behavior that you resent right now. But Rome wasn't built in a day, and neither will your new set of skills be.

When people refuse to look at your point of view, you need to let them know that what they're doing isn't okay—that you understand it, you see through it, and you're above it. This chapter will highlight how a change in attitude can begin to transform your way of relating to your obstinate family, friends, or associates, regardless of their position in your personal life or in your workplace. This is where the fun begins!

You may have been asking yourself, "Why me? Why do I have to be the one to carry the burden of getting them to stop being difficult with me? Why won't they just grow up—again, and better this time? Why can't they just change by themselves?" Since the future will always have in it difficult people who refuse to see things your way, you might as well just accept the fact that they won't and move on.

TAKE STOCK OF YOUR BAD HABITS

Do you want to level the playing field? If you do, it's up to you to do some homework about some of your own habits first.

Bad habits are interesting things to consider. How does one get them? It seems as though people grow them. They stem from different feelings about and responses to situations. They're self-replicating. Before we know it, people are stuck in their same old patterns with nowhere else to go.

Habits are not easy things to break. Most people still have to curb the impulse to reach for a very large bag of peanut M&Ms,

a martini, or some other indulgence when they are in stressful situations, even though they have made the decision not to do so.

Up until now, you may have been merely coping with difficult people, repeating behaviors that you have learned, whether they were effective or not. There is good news, however; as soon as you become aware of your bad habits, you can do something about them. So take some time now to review this list of bad habits to which most people can relate all too well. Be honest with yourself. Think of this as a self-awareness quiz to help you recognize what you do when dealing with those people who refuse to or can't see it your way.

When you are dealing with difficult people, do you

1. Automatically take a subservient position?
2. Say to yourself, "I'm probably overreacting"?
3. Immediately assume a caretaking role?
4. Convince yourself that if you did confront, you'd probably lose?
5. Become too aggressive?
6. Constantly decide that it's not worth it?
7. Ignore the cues that tell you it's time to back off?
8. Tell yourself that you're taking it too seriously?
9. Worry that other people will blame you for any upheaval?
10. Immediately feel the need to walk all over them?
11. Worry about them not liking you?
12. Go for the cheap shot, because something is better than nothing?
13. Wish that you could be more like them?
14. Act personal instead of personable?
15. Tell them off on a regular basis?
16. Never ask for what you want?

17. Use pouting or withdrawing to soften them up?
18. Run hot and cold by being inconsistent with your reactions?
19. Share the reasons for your mood swings with anyone who'll listen?
20. Act like a victim when you don't get your way?
21. Ignore difficult behavior, hoping it will go away by itself?
22. Wait so long to deal with something that you let it blow up out of proportion?
23. Keep hoping that difficult people will see the error of their ways without your having to confront them?
24. Use helplessness as your ultimate weapon?

Did any of your answers come as a surprise to you? Were you aware of what you have been doing with difficult, unyielding people?

There is an expression that you may have heard many times from many different sources: "The way you were raised is your parents' fault. If you stay that way, it's your own." In other words, you have choices. You can stick with and hide behind these bad habits, or you can refine them to better reflect who you are now and who you want to be. As you go through this book, the tools and techniques you will read about will act as replacement parts; so, for instance, instead of acting like a victim when you don't get your way (number 20), you'll be able to realign your reactions and do some strategic planning. You'll tell yourself that even though you didn't get your way this time, next time you'll be ready with a new attitude, a new approach, and some hot new maneuvers.

When you acknowledge that you have these bad habits, you will already be on the road to recovery, even though you know that merely to acknowledge something does almost nothing to actually change it. For this, you need to make the commitment to work on changing yourself by changing what you do.

Which brings you to the first change: stepping out of your comfort zone, where your bad habits reside. Bad habits are comfort-zone keepers. They lull you into believing that just because something is familiar, it is helpful. Not true. Just because "you've always done it this way" doesn't make it the best way to go. Here's an example.

Perhaps you've gotten really good at number 15 on the bad-habits list: telling people off on a regular basis. This can feel great when you do it, but telling off your nemeses makes them even more determined to make your life miserable. If you tell them off because you let yourself get to the boiling point instead of dealing with their difficult behavior one incident at a time, you'll never win the difficult-person war.

CHOOSE TO BE ON TOP

One of the biggest mistakes that you may make is to treat problems with antagonists different from the way you treat most other problems. When you are having difficulty with other people at work, for instance, begin by answering the following questions:

1. How would you define the problem?
2. Are you willing to work on it?
3. What would it look like "fixed"?
4. Are your expectations realistic?

These questions help set the tone for keeping your position on top. Being on top means planning instead of reacting. It means observing instead of feeling victimized. It means making choices based on information and gut feelings. But you've got to be willing to stop and take the time to do this—and to listen to your answers.

Norm applied this question-and-answer technique in a recent experience. As a child and then as a young man, he had little self-confidence. But after he was passed over for a promotion, he took personal-development classes in assertiveness training, and as a result of this tremendous infusion of information and support, he went to the opposite end of the spectrum. For a while, he admits he could have put an "explosives" sign on his forehead and everyone would have agreed. Instead of defining a problem, finding out whether or not people were willing to work on it, visualizing it fixed, and making sure his expectations weren't unrealistic, he attacked.

To say that people would grip their chairs after he opened his mouth would be an understatement. He learned this by judging others' reactions to him when he came on too strong, too soon. This was particularly apparent once in a presentation that he was making for a professional association. In front of two hundred people, one person stood up and told him that he was sounding "very hostile." The room became so quiet you could hear a pin drop. All eyes were either on him or looking down. He couldn't believe it, even though the person was probably right about his demeanor. It was embarrassing and humiliating, and Norm was ticked! After the shock wore off, he thought about how to respond.

Here is the thought process that Norm went through.

"At first, I wanted to 'thank him for the illuminating moment,' then I wanted to ask him if he enjoyed using me for target practice in front of all those people. I also wanted to ask him if he was uneducated or just very stupid. I finally decided to smile and say, 'Thank you. I appreciate your honesty. I am strong, and sometimes it shows more than necessary.'" More silence, and then applause. He had turned the other people in the group into his allies. The audience was his, and there was no more heckling.

Being on top doesn't mean being more sarcastic than others. It doesn't necessarily mean saying things like "Someone like you would say something like that." It doesn't even mean insulting a difficult person by saying "You don't sweat much for such a large, hairy person." It means changing your perspective and adjusting your behavior so that you feel strong, upright, and powerful. Norm did this by clarifying exactly what the problem was, deciding that he was willing to address it, allowing himself to fantasize, and then pulling himself back to reality.

Take a moment to look around the room you are sitting in right now; from your vantage point, it looks one way. Stand on a chair and you will see a very different sight. Kneel on the floor and the room changes again. The view you get from standing on the chair gives you a broader perspective that is more expansive. Plain and simple, things look different from up there on top.

STOP "SHOULDING" ON YOURSELF

Several years ago, Helene and three other department heads in her—all male—firm were discussing how to divide up a new office site. Helene said nothing as one man after another selected all the offices that had windows, leaving one dark room that resembled a closet and three cubicles for Helene and her staff. After the meeting, when asked how satisfied she was with the outcome, Helene said that she was angry, disgusted, and disappointed. She hated the office space that she and her staff would be forced to occupy. She thought that her feelings should have been considered. It never occurred to her that in order to consider her feelings and take them seriously, other people had to know what they were. She spent the next week "shoulding" on herself and the other three department heads: "I should have gotten more." "They should have thought about my needs." "They should have asked me what I wanted." "They shouldn't have been so selfish and pushy."

It was pointed out that these men were difficult because she allowed them to be. They did what worked for them as she had said nothing and had never let them know their actions were not what she wanted. She could have stated her wishes, disagreed with their plan, and negotiated for what she wanted. The other men (a) were not mind readers, (b) experienced no resistance and so went full steam ahead with what they wanted, and (c) probably congratulated themselves on pulling one over on her. She kept on saying to me, "Well, it wasn't worth fighting about." What she was doing was depriving herself of what she wanted by blaming the situation on them, and the three difficult men didn't even have to be nasty or pushy. She gave herself a double whammy, because not only did she inflict the pain and have to deal with it, she then proceeded to blame herself for doing it. How exhausting, demoralizing, and counterproductive!

Shoulding on yourself takes many forms. You know you're doing it when once again you find yourself having that same conversation with the steering wheel on your drive home. Or you suddenly become aware that you are mutilating the produce in the grocery store when you stop to buy something for dinner after a meeting from hell with a difficult person.

Shoulding on yourself means that you are using hindsight to reprimand yourself for not having had the foresight to do or say something at a given time. This is a ridiculous thing to do;

shoulding on yourself is a futile exercise. It would be much more productive to say, "If I ever find myself in a situation like that again, what could I say and what could I do differently that would be more gratifying and constructive?"

When you eliminate "I should have said," "I can't believe I said," "If only I had said," and "Why didn't I say" and substitute "What could I say to get what I want" and "What would I say to feel powerful, true to myself, and clear" you are finally starting to move in the right direction.

STOP LIMITING, START BUILDING

To change the way people treat you, you have to be honest with yourself regarding the messages you may be putting out that are making you an easy target. What behaviors are you using that are undermining your equality potential?

The more information you have to work with, the more you can do what you need to do to effect the changes you want.

Take a moment to answer these questions, and when you do, think about yourself. Don't just think about your answers; write them down.

1. If you were describing yourself to a person you think respects you and who often sees things your way, what would you say? Consider how you would like to be seen by this person. Write the exact words that you would use.
2. Now, if you were describing yourself to a person you think does not respect you and has never seen anything of significance your way, what would you say? Consider how you would like to be seen by this person. Write the exact words that you would use.

Now read what you've written. Are there some differences in your answers? Probably so. People tend to present themselves differently to those from whom they get respect. It is part of everyone's conditioning, and most people don't even realize what they are doing. What did you learn about yourself? What are your best characteristics? Did either one of your answers reflect these characteristics fully? Chances are, combining both answers would provide the best picture of who you are. Anything less is incomplete. You have to stop limiting yourself when you show the world who you are, and you have to start building yourself so that you can create the person you want to be.

To help you understand your self-defeating patterns, here's an example of how Peter answered the questions in a management training seminar.

For question number one, he described himself as flexible, open, eager, and willing to learn; and for question number two, he said that he was dynamic, a fast learner, and smart. Is the difference jumping off the page at you? Peter used passive words to describe himself to the person he believed valued what he had to offer and stepped into the more assertive domain for the person who did not respect his input. He showed himself as being more open and flexible and in a learning mode in the first case because he felt he had nothing to prove. In the second case, he tried to come across as more assertive to establish himself as being a contributor. This process of sometimes trying to overcompensate and other times coming across as too naïve can be one of those bad habits that will be discussed more later in this chapter. Really think about this for a moment; it's an insidious tendency, and that's what makes it so destructive.

Go back and look at how you responded to the questions. How did you come across? Did you tend to come across stronger in the relationships you have with some people and weaker in your relationships with others? A lot of people do. It is part of the cultural training mentioned earlier. Or, you may be one of those people who seem to walk around with a chain saw when there is a person who does not see things your way within fifty yards of them. This is not unusual. Many people believe that the best defense is a strong offense. Although this may be true, there is such a thing as going too far, being a little too intense, or coming across as too negative.

Balance: That's what this is all about. Balance has to do with the way you behave based on the way you feel and your attitudes about yourself. You can come across as too passive or too aggressive when you really need to be assertive. How do you choose the right place to be and the right mix of behaviors so that you feel true to yourself and present a true picture to the challenging people in your work life? Examine your attitudes.

POLITE PEOPLE DO TALK BACK

Many of the tactics that will be talked about in the upcoming chapters may sound very different from those you usually resort to when dealing with difficult people, and, as a result, your immediate reaction may be to toss them off, thinking "I could never say that" or "I could never do that." Try not to let negativity or self-consciousness get in the way of your progress. If you are willing to take some small risks, you will learn that in fact you are very strong, much stronger than you have ever given yourself credit for. Every day will present more interesting opportunities for you to get people to see things your way.

And while you are using your new skills, each difficult person you test them on will see an outer image of control; so even if you're falling apart on the inside, it will be your secret. It won't show, and there is no one to give it away! Composure is an interesting phenomenon; it can look one way and feel another. When facing a resistant person, it is important to behave as if you feel calm. You always have time to fall apart in private, later, and the more you try your new behaviors and get positive results, the faster your fear will subside and the less falling apart you'll do.

Little feels worse than being taken advantage of, and you know that you're not alone in having this feeling. Most people hate it when others don't care about how they feel or what they want, and they get upset with themselves for allowing it to happen, especially if it is a pattern that repeats itself. True, you sometimes get tired of being the one who has to establish the boundaries in a relationship, and it can be exhausting to have to ride shotgun for yourself; but, hey, what's the alternative?

What can get discouraging is the recognition that for every difficult person whose behavior they neutralize, at least ten or twenty more lie in wait, and the supply is endless. There is a silver lining to this cloud, however, if you think of this glut as a never-ending supply of difficult people on which to try all the new techniques you are about to learn.

As a friend of mine says, "Having a relationship with difficult and demanding people that is give-and-take doesn't mean that I give and that they always get to take."

What's the point of all this? The point is that polite people really do talk back; they just do it respectfully. Polite people don't try to "outsmart" those they find difficult by sounding rough and tough. Polite people do talk to express rather than impress, and they do this partly to keep difficult people focused on watching the front door, while they slip in the side.

Cut to the chase. Polite people do talk back—and they do it with style!

The first step in changing your behavior toward difficult people is to adjust your attitude. The following list of actions will help. You may already practice some of them routinely. If so, that's great. It will give you time to think about and act on those that are new to you.

1. Recognize that your attitude is in your hands, and if you've been putting it in someone else's hands, now is the time to take it back, immediately.
2. See yourself the way you want to be, and always remember to start every single day with that healthy mental picture.
3. Stop worrying about what other people think. A lot of them hardly ever do think, and when they do, it's probably an underwhelming experience anyway.
4. Give yourself permission to make a fool of yourself. Perfection is boring and, when taken to extremes, can become obsessive. Don't waste energy fixing what's not broken.
5. Decide that it's okay to laugh at yourself. Look for the humor in tough situations with difficult people. The worst situations usually make the best stories later; the more awkward experiences you have, the funnier you'll be at your next gathering.
6. Decide that it's okay—no, wonderful—to ask for help from someone who's "been there." Others sometimes know exactly how to assist and are often willing to advise you. Adjust your "I am an island" behavior.

7. Resolve to act the part and see what happens. When you try acting in control of yourself, you will find that you remain in control of yourself. What a feeling!

8. Acknowledge your fear, feel your fear, but don't fail to try because of your fear.

Only you can control your attitude. The adjustment switch belongs on the inside, not on the outside, where you've been allowing people who dismiss your ideas to mess with it.

POWER IS NOT A BAD WORD

Your attitude about yourself is closely related to how you feel about being powerful. Chapter 1 focused on the power of difficult people. Now it's time to talk about *your* power, because if you don't recognize it, you won't use it.

Look in the mirror. Do you resemble your idea of how a powerful and influential person should look? Maybe you ought to back up a few steps and ask yourself what power really means and why you have such a hard time owning and using it. What are your beliefs about power? Here is an opportunity to make a quick spot check. Keep in mind that power, like beauty, is in the eye of the beholder. The phrase "all that glitters is not gold" also relates to the perception of power—meaning that what one person sees as power, another may not.

Do you think each of the following statements is true or false?

1. If you feel powerful, you'll look powerful.

2. The one who has the loudest voice and quickest tongue will have the most power.

3. Anyone can acquire power.

4. You can only be powerful if you are credible.

5. Power is something you can lose, and once you lose it, it is gone forever.

6. Men are automatically more powerful than women.

7. Information is power, and you can use it to control people and situations.

8. Confidence is power, and you can't be powerful without it.

9. Endurance is power: You need to last longer than anyone else.

10. Experience is power if the experience has been good.

11. Powerful people are automatically cold and insensitive to others.

12. The person who wins the argument has more power the next time.

As you read these statements about power, how did you respond?

ITEM 1: True. Your confidence usually shapes what people see, except when you use self-defeating behaviors or words that undermine your presence.

ITEM 2: False. A loud voice usually suggests that the person is out of control, reacting emotionally instead of logically and playing too many cards too soon.

ITEM 3: True. Here are just a few of the sources of power: Your position at work or in your family; your ability to negatively impact (really scare or threaten) another person; your ability to give people what they want, emotionally or otherwise; charisma, or a sparkling personality that another person finds charming and engaging;

your possession of information that another person wants or needs; and last but not least, your personal connections to others (for example, you're tight with their boss).

How many of these sources of power do you currently possess, and are you taking advantage of them? Don't underestimate their usefulness in dealing with difficult people. Although they can all be invaluable, one problem many people have is the idea that using any kind of power is manipulative and therefore bad. This attitude, pounded into so many people early on, accounts for their unwillingness to stand tall and be counted.

When Chris, a personal fitness trainer, walked into a room full of businessmen whom she was supposed to lead in a physical workout, she got to utilize a few sources of power. Listen to her recount of what happened:

> Imagine me, six feet tall, blonde, and—I'll say so myself—looking great, in tremendous physical condition, walking into the room wearing hot pink spandex workout clothes. I could just see all those guys thinking, "What is that?" and then fixating on the fact that I was blonde and female and concluding, "Bimbette." It was really quite amazing to watch. When I announced it was time to get started, one guy actually stood up to work out with a lit cigar in his mouth. It took no time for me to demonstrate my strength. In front of his cronies and with a big smile on my

face, before he even knew what hit him, I picked him up two feet off the ground and carried him to the door, where I deposited him and said, "You can't smoke that thing in here." I then proceeded to demonstrate the various activities the group would be doing, and just for the heck of it, I bench-pressed a few hundred pounds. Needless to say, every man in the group behaved himself for the rest of that session, and nobody dared light a cigar or anything else for the rest of the week.

Chris did two things. First, we have acknowledge that she did descend to the macho level and beat the guy at his own game. Not every woman can or wants to do that, but in this instance, it worked for her. She also used a combination of her experience, skill, and charisma to tame this group of difficult people. Their bimbette impression totally disappeared as soon as she lifted the cigar-smoking guy in the air. Her dry wit and willingness to play with them made it easy for them to look at her differently and enjoy her personality. She proved herself and made herself approachable with one quick interaction.

ITEM 4: True. Credibility really means that you have to be genuine, not necessarily the best or the brightest. If people think you're lying, they will not respond well.

ITEM 5: False. Every day brings a new opportunity to try a different approach. Some days you might be more powerful, others less. There is no "forever" as regards power.

ITEM 6:   False. What a bunch of bull! Women who are raised
to feel and be competent and self-confident can match
men step for step, move for move, and if a woman
wasn't raised that way, as soon as she recognizes the
void, she can raise herself retroactively.

ITEM 7:   True. And although it is counterproductive, it must be
acknowledged that withholding information is also a
form of power.

ITEM 8:   False. Not true. You can fake it. The well-known
phrase used in commercials about never letting the
other people see you sweat refers to this notion. You
can use the right words and the right behaviors to
create the confident appearance you need.

ITEM 9:   True. But only if you can wear them down, and this
sometimes incurs backlash, which is not so good.

ITEM 10:   True. But only half the truth. Bad experience can also
make you wiser and better prepared than anyone else.

ITEM 11:   False. They can be, but the two issues are not related,
and, in fact, powerful people often use their power to
help others.

ITEM 12:   False. Each situation is different, and you have to let
go of past issues.

Has all this changed your mind about you and power? It is
important that you no longer believe that power is a scarce
resource that you either have or always wish for. Power does not
have to be a threatening or elusive phenomenon. It can be had
and enjoyed by all, so why not by you?

In chapters 4 and 5, we talk more about power moves that you can make and when to make them; but, in the meantime, ask yourself the following questions about power:

1. Do you use it?
2. What could you do right now to take advantage of what you've got and be more powerful?
3. When will you try a new way of being powerful?

When you take a risk, you will find out that it will pay off.

THEY DON'T HAVE TO LIKE IT

One of the most valuable bits of information for you to know about changing your attitude and dealing with people who don't see it your way is something Nicole learned one Saturday morning. Her husband, Max, who is a wonderful but disorganized person, walked into the kitchen, looked at Nicole impatiently, and asked, "Where's the hammer?" "The hammer?" Nicole repeated. "I think it's in the toolbox." Max looked at Nicole with an incredulous expression on his face, as if she had just said something horribly nasty, and boomed, "Nicole, where's the hammer?" Nicole thought to herself, "Maybe he couldn't hear me," so she repeated, "It's in the toolbox." Judging from Max's reaction, Nicole was wrong.

Now, after the two had finished "discussing" the whereabouts of the hammer loudly enough for all the neighbors to hear, Nicole finally broke the code. "Where's the hammer?" really meant "Go get the hammer and bring it to me." All right, Nicole thought when it was all over and she had cooled down, I can learn how to do this. If the game is played this way, I'm ready for it.

Two weeks later, after a long day at the office for both of them, they ended up back in the kitchen. As they finished sorting the mail, Max looked at the clock and said, "No wonder I'm so hungry, it's 7:30." Nicole knew the code, and she was ready! Instead of saying, "Dinner? I've just spent two hours in traffic, I'm exhausted, and you want me to make dinner?" her response was, "Oh, I am too." As she went off to change her clothes, she casually turned back and asked Max to make the same dinner for her that he was planning on preparing for himself. (She later found out that the menu was cheese and crackers.)

Does this sound totally foreign to you? Are you looking forward to trying something like it, or thinking that you could never be so bold as to displease somebody? Are you horrified at the way Nicole handled it? If you're stuck because you're concerned about displeasing somebody, you need to look at what your concerns are and what you think will happen if you respond differently.

Carol checked into the resort hotel in which her company was holding its annual strategic planning session. She arrived a day early because of the difference in airfare. The weather was hot and humid. When she was shown to her room, she was horrified to find that it was dark and musty, full of mold and mildew. Just standing on the carpet for two minutes resulted in about eight fleabites on her feet and ankles. While making her way back to the check-in desk, she noticed several lovely rooms with marble floors and freshly painted walls. She complained to the male clerk about her room and requested one of the others. The clerk shook his head in a "there, there" way and smiled. It was impossible to change her room because all the others were already reserved. She shook her head and smiled, too. Then, she leaned over the desk and countered, "I have a free day. I have nowhere to go and nothing to do, so I'll gladly stand here and wait until one becomes available." "You can't do that," the clerk objected. "You'll have to step aside. We have a lot of other people checking in today." "Oh, that's okay," she told him. "Since I'm not moving, you can just talk and work around me." And with that, she leaned even more comfortably on the desk, opened her laptop, smiled up at him, and began to work. She had her new room within five minutes. Needless to say, she did not bond with the reception clerk, but she didn't have to. She was crossing this hotel off her company's list.

Now, what about your relationships at work? It really helps if people, at the least, don't mind being around you. Love you? Not important. Want to invite you home to dinner? Uh-uh. Retch or seethe at the thought of talking to you? Here, you have a problem.

Some people seem to carry an axe around with them and use it whenever they encounter the least bit of resistance. You know the type, and maybe you are the type. They squash an ant with a hammer. True, work is not a popularity contest, but there is such a thing as consistently coming on too strong. Remember, you don't want to destroy resistant or hostile people; you just want to change the relationships you have with them, and the next chapter will help you do just that.

4

SKILLS FOR

THRIVING

Some of the change-producing techniques in this chapter may be totally new to you, and some you may have used extensively, but never consciously, as tools for dealing with those who can't or are unwilling to see it your way. As you read those ideas that are very different from those to which you're accustomed, be aware of your own resistance, the "yes, buts" that you'll inevitably come up with. So many people are afraid to change the status quo, to make the moves, to walk the walk and talk the talk that will assist them in getting to a new place. It is not easy to grow, and sometimes it is downright uncomfortable, but you should know that by resisting change, you're erecting your own barriers and helping your antagonists keep you right where they want you. Don't do it! Since you already know that you can change difficult people's behavior by starting with your own, resolve to do it and move forward.

Learn to Use a Foreign Language: Body Language

Begin by focusing on body language, which for most is a foreign language that anyone can easily learn to speak, control, and use to his or her advantage.

One picture is worth a thousand words, and your body language provides volumes of information for your opponents to read and use against you. A shopping mall, an office, a conference, a theater lobby, a bus, or any public place is a perfect spot for testing this idea. The next time you have a moment or two, take a good look around and check out people around you, keeping two things in mind. First, how are they dressed? This is important, since this is the package that body language is wrapped in. Do they look serious, credible, appealing, seductive, professional, confident, easy on the eyes, flashy, babyish, cheap, or anything else? Whatever you decide is okay, although it is not a good idea to go up to them and share your opinions. Don't stop there with these preliminary observations. Look again. How much of the image they project is the clothing they're wearing and how much is the way they carry themselves, their gestures, their posture, or the physical space they keep between them and anyone they might be with? Now check them out one more time. If they are in conversations with other people, what are they doing? Do they make direct eye contact? Are their arms folded; are their hands in their pockets, on their hips, on the other person's hips (just kidding), where? All of these gestures are important since they give the people you are trying to deal with signals about what they can or cannot get away with.

So that you will learn enough about body language to do it justice, here's a map to follow. The face is our first stop, because it is the area that can contain or give away the most. Brenda, a lawyer, fondly remembers when a tough business associate with whom she had just clinched a deal remarked to her, "You know, when you smile, you look absolutely harmless; nobody can see the horns." She chuckles every time she repeats this remark, because she knows that working on using her smile has not taken that long but has continually brought great benefits in all areas of her life.

John, on the other hand, remembers his constant frustration when his difficult boss, after telling him to do something, used to say to him, "I know you don't want to do it, and this is just another example of your bad attitude." John's boss had read his facial expression and been able to see how he was feeling and apparently what he was thinking. This was not a good situation, since she ended up firing John before he had lined up a new job.

When choosing your facial expressions, pay attention to how you want to appear to each challenging person, and then monitor his or her reactions and comments. Establish eye contact without squinting, glaring, or looking wide-eyed and overwhelmed. Smile, but not too broadly. Use a medium smile so that you look neither too controlled nor too bubbly. Don't flare your nostrils. A lot of people have this habit without realizing it, and it's counterproductive for two reasons. The first is that it is not particularly pleasant to look up someone's nostrils (and as a short person, you'd be amazed at what you see up there!). And the second is that it clearly shows your tension level, and that's nobody's business except yours, unless you decide to share it with them. (Of course, you don't care if the other person does it, since it will give you more information about their anger and stress levels.)

And what about lips? Licking or biting them, corners turned up, corners turned down, pursed tightly together—each of these gives a clear sign about what you are thinking and exactly how you are feeling.

Some people blush more than others. Blushing can be a real problem when you're in a tough situation with adversaries; it is like having a neon sign on your forehead flashing messages like "out of control," "panicked," "shy," "sexually attracted," and "uh-oh," to name a few. If you're an involuntary blusher, don't worry; you will get over it as you develop your communication, confrontation, and positioning skills.

It goes without saying that everything you need to be aware of on your own face is also exactly what you need to look for when talking to or observing the face of another person. Put all the facial clues into some kind of perspective, however; don't just take one observation and isolate it. For example, a difficult man licking his lips can mean lust, nervousness, or preparation to pounce (verbally, not physically). It can even mean leftover crumbs from lunch, so watch it!

Chris, the six-foot-tall fitness trainer talked about earlier, uses her smile to disarm difficult men in business transactions, because they make the mistake of thinking they can take advantage of the fact that she's a woman. When she wants the advantage, she smiles a lot and tilts her head, which is very confusing to them because they get mixed messages. Is she a very assertive woman or the stereotypical dumb blonde? Her response to this? "You think I'm a dumb blonde? Right, good, keep thinking that." She laughs at the concept of dumb blondes because she finally figured out that the word *dumb* really should be applied to the behavior of the people who make assumptions about blondes, not to the blondes themselves. A refreshing attitude from a very secure, very tall woman who could have had all sorts of complexes from growing up in a society that says that girls (and women) are supposed to be shorter, weaker, and more petite than boys (and men).

There are a few other body-language faux pas exhibited by both genders. You see them every day in your work world. Aside from rounded shoulders, no-neck tortoise posture, glaring or staring, smirking, bodies half turned away and fidgeting with anything within reach, here are the worst ones, the ones that give other people the upper hand in about two seconds:

THE LIMP WRIST: You've seen it. The arm is bent in a right angle, the elbow is against the body between the chest and the waist, and the fingers are pointing down. The arm looks as if it's in a sling, but there is no sling.

THE PIGEON-TOED POSITION: People look at this one and see, "Attack me (verbally), because I am an easy target. I'll probably just fall over, because my knees will knock and throw me off balance." Plus, pigeon toes for some reason seem to accompany fidgeting fingers, a dead giveaway for nervousness.

THE BREAST-PROTECTOR LOOK: This one, with the arms folded over the chest, is particularly interesting. On people with large chests or stomachs, it looks as if their arms are sitting on or under a shelf. The message, when accompanied by a scowl, is often "Don't even think of coming near me." If accompanied by a weak smile or the head tilted to one side, it is "I'm scared, and I'm protecting myself from you because I know that you are stronger than I am."

THE BIRD-HEAD LOOK: This is the one where people tilt their heads to one side, thus making themselves look a lot like sparrows listening and waiting for who-knows-what. Most people don't associate sparrows with strength or the notion of forces to be reckoned with.

THE HANDS-ON-HIPS POSITION: This usually transmits the message "I am ticked, and if I take my hands off my hips, I'll probably wrap them around your throat." It immediately gives away the fact that someone has gotten to you and made you angry. Not good.

SITTING OR STANDING WITH LEGS APART: When women do this wearing pants, it's not great but not terrible, either; in a skirt, it can be a real problem. When men do it, the message is that they are not really engaged in what is going on.

FIRING WITH THE TRIGGER FINGER: This maneuver—pointing at the other person with your index finger, usually aiming at their face or chest—is accusatory and attacking and usually results in a defensive response.

Watching others' body language is as important as mastering your own. The pelvic thrust usually suggests that someone's focus is as much on you as it is on what they are saying. It tells you that they are trying to make an impression and that they want you to pay a lot of attention to them. Another common exhibition of body language is the more aggressive stance, which often includes repeated finger pointing, sharp hand and arm movements, or leaning forward on both hands across the desk or table. A steely glare, very serious frown, or eye-rolling are also big power moves. Don't be intimidated or put off by any of these. Watch it when it is happening, and say to yourself, "I can deal with this." Distance yourself emotionally. When someone with whom you are speaking smirks, tilts his or her head back, and shakes it from side to side, you know that you are wasting your time if you keep on talking. You have to stop and change the dynamics of the interaction because the individual is telling you that what you are saying is foolish or wrong. Closely related to this, but somewhat different, is when someone sits with the head tilted backward, looking, you think, at the ceiling. This person would like you to leave and has actually made you disappear by shifting his or her gaze.

There are also those body-language moves that some people still use at work today because they refuse to acknowledge the sexual harassment rules and regulations. You all know the "I'm just a hugging kind of guy or gal," or the person who has assumed the role of official office neck-and-back massager for all coworkers. This body language—touching people without their permission and assuming that they like it—demonstrates the adversary's tendency to invade another person's space. When a difficult person travels into your space without a passport, get ready to move or to use your own facial expression to stake out your territory. Don't say anything nasty. You can even make a joke of it to lighten the tension and say, "Wait a second, Joe, when you sit or stand so close, my eyes cross and I can't see you."

Let's say you do feel tense when you are talking to difficult people. Since you don't want to let them see how you feel, you know for certain that biting your nails or gnawing on your fists is not recommended. (Biting their nails or gnawing on their fists is also definitely not recommended.) One of the best hand gestures is the steeple position—hands in front of you with all ten fingertips touching, forming a V. Doing this, you can push your fingers together to do something with the tension. If you are sitting, make sure that you keep the small of your back pressed against the back of your chair to prevent you from leaning or lunging forward, since this would show your intense reaction and desire to push your point. Don't recline way back, which would demonstrate your desire to get away from them because they have succeeded in making you feel vulnerable.

Many people dealing with difficult individuals undermine themselves constantly because they've only learned how to put on a happy face and friendly demeanor instead of wearing a poker face and a neutrally positioned body.

Many years ago, as a fairly new computer consultant presenting a course to a group of several hundred accountants, Ellen made the mistake of wearing just a skirt with a silky blouse. It was very cold in the room, and she was nervous. Ten minutes into her talk, she noticed that no one in the room was looking at her face. When she realized why, it became apparent that to scrape together any shred of dignity, she had to keep one arm across her chest while writing and pointing with the other. She looked anything but in control. Needless to say, ever since that time she has never given a presentation without a jacket. Make sure that you are prepared for whatever you might have to deal with in the body-language department.

You still have a lot of changes to make at home and in the workplace. Begin by packaging yourself effectively, taking advantage of your control over your body language, and using your ability to read the body language of others.

LISTEN TO WHAT THEY'RE SAYING AND TO WHAT THEY'RE NOT

Fine-tuning your listening skills is not unlike wearing a bullet-proof vest. It enables you to project confidence: "I can hear you, I can see you, and I can engage with you, but you can't control me."

Gerda, a very effective senior executive who works with difficult people all the time, enjoys listening. It provides her the opportunity to "let the train run on by" when she knows that nothing she can say will make them really stop and listen. "I can get hit by the train if I step in front of it, so instead, I step aside, watch it pass, and then decide my next move."

Chuck puts it a little differently: "I listen; it's as if I'm lying in wait. Like a battleship. I know my time will come." He's right, too!

Sometimes, when you really listen to what a difficult person is saying, you hear amazing things, and you discover why you've gotten trapped so often in the past. You realize that what you are hearing when they ask an apparently innocent question is really what many people refer to as QWAP, "questions with answers provided." These are not really questions, and there are no right answers except theirs. That's why you can never win in these situations. You think that there is something else on the table for discussion, but the other person has no such agenda. Becoming aware of this will help you avoid needless, angry, dead-end discussions. Some examples might be:

"Don't you think it's too late to submit a proposal?"

"You aren't going to wear that, are you?"

"You don't really think that will work, do you?"

Just how important is listening? Lucy wanted to sell her handcrafted jewelry and contacted a department-store buyer who was approached by hundreds of people a year. Before the meeting, she added up all her costs, which totaled $40 per piece of jewelry. She was nervous because she thought she would be asking too much and pricing herself out of the market. When she finally had her face-to-face meeting with the buyer, the buyer breezed in twenty minutes late, looked at her watch, sat down, and showed her difficult-person boredom with a sneering "I'm too busy to give you a lot of my time" look. Before Lucy could get a word out, the buyer immediately took over the meeting and began telling her about all the problems the department store would have with her necklaces, specifically the packaging they'd have to do and the display challenges they'd face. As Lucy was listening to the buyer, she began thinking about how she could reduce her costs. She was getting entirely too wrapped up in her own thoughts, but luckily she allowed herself to tune back into the buyer and what she was saying. Lucy was shaking inside when all of sudden the buyer said, "So, in light of all this, I'd only be able to offer you $75 apiece." Lucy almost fell off her chair.

Listening is very powerful; when done well, it can really give you an edge.

Here is an opportunity to take stock of your listening habits. Grade yourself on the following behaviors, keeping in mind what happens to you when a person you are having trouble with begins doing their troublesome thing. This is not about how you listen to a friend or someone with whom you have a healthy relationship. It is about what happens to your listening habits in an emotionally charged or deference-based encounter.

For each of the following behaviors, grade yourself according to this scale:

A = Always
B = Almost always
C = Rarely
D = Never

1. I allow the other person to finish a sentence and/or complete a thought before I begin to respond.
2. I listen to what the other person really means, whether his or her words are actually saying it.
3. I make myself stay focused on what others say, even if I am repulsed by something they've already done or because they remind me of another cantankerous person.
4. I ignore distractions and tune out everything around me and listen only to the other person.
5. I look and sound as if I am interested in and considering what the other person is saying.

How did you do? The more A's, the better.

Let's take a look at each of these techniques and discuss why they are so effective.

NUMBER 1: Not cutting someone off too soon is important for several reasons, the main one being that you won't get all the information he or she might be willing to give you. Lucy the jeweler is a good example of this. The other reason is that you already know what you have to say, and you need to take the time to really hear what the other person has to say.

If you are an extrovert you probably need to pay particular attention to this technique, and if you do cut the other person off, a good comeback would be "Excuse me, I got so interested in what you were saying that I jumped ahead of myself." Then really listen by making yourself count to ten (to yourself) between the time the other person closes his or her mouth and you open yours.

NUMBER 2:   Listening between the lines is something that has been discussed before. For example, when your boss says, "I'm not sure your idea would work," this often means something like "If I say yes to you, Joe and Fred will be upset, and I don't want to deal with that." You have to be willing to check out what you think the other person might mean and pay particular attention to whether or not you are really being told no.

NUMBER 3:   Try to get beyond your reactions of anger, dislike, or disgust. Listen to each person and regard what is being said as a brand-new opportunity to gather the information you need, not as a time to "once again be subjected to garbage I can't use and don't want to ever hear again."

NUMBER 4:   Ignoring distractions is a matter of focusing. The more you listen, the more the other person gives; and the more you're given, the better off you are. Here is your opportunity to practice your creative and con-trolled use of facial expressions. Show interest with eye contact and body language. Look relaxed and appear interested by not falling asleep or striking an on-guard position.

NUMBER 5:   Showing interest has to do with faking it. You have to work hard to find some shred of information to keep your interest, even if it is only your amazement at what the other person is saying or trying to do. It sometimes helps if you think of yourself as an anthropologist, listening intently to understand this interesting specimen.

What is the upshot of all this? Go back and look at your responses to all these items. The more you practice these five listening habits, the better a listener you will be. You do have to think before you open your mouth, and the only true way to think sharply is to listen to what the other person is saying, implying, or not saying by holding back.

When your emotions are revved up, your perceptions are skewed. You say things that you mean, you just don't mean to say them. You disclose information you would not normally disclose if you were calm. If you work on listening more and speaking impulsively less, you won't have as many disclosure regrets.

There is a time to speak up and a time to clam up. When you decide to clam up, also decide to listen up. Punctuate your listening with affirming techniques that will appeal to the egos of contrary people. Throw in the occasional, "Uh-huh," "I see," or the Johnny Carson special, "I didn't know that." Difficult people love this stuff, and it often encourages them.

With three magic words, "Isn't that interesting?" you can get them to give you more information than you ever imagined. Nod, smile if appropriate to express pleasure, and maintain eye contact. Repeat in your own words some of what they've said ("So you think that I have been spending too much time with my friends?") and listen to them excitedly say, "Yes, because," and then spill the beans about what's really bothering them.

Listening is one part of communicating and dealing effectively with difficult people. Another is talking. A critical step is the way you ask for information—questioning effectively.

GET THE INFORMATION YOU NEED WITHOUT GETTING THEIR GOAT

If you listen really well when the other person is talking, you'll have the opportunity to ask the crucial questions. Please note that "Are you crazy?" or "You're kidding, aren't you?" or "How long have you been delusionary?" aren't the kinds of questions to keep in mind.

To prepare yourself, read the following questions and answer them without thinking too much.

1. How old are you?
2. What are some of your fondest vacation memories?
3. How hard is it for you to get up in the morning?
4. What kinds of things do you do best?
5. What time does your workday end?

Questions 1 and 5 are commonly referred to as closed questions. They get answers that are focused and specific. You probably replied with a number (or maybe "None of your business") to question number 1 and a number (or "Not soon enough") to number 5. Questions 2, 3, and 4 are known as open questions. You probably thought more about these and began to recall more information in response to them. This is because open questions are nonrestrictive. They can eliminate boundaries and encourage dialogue. Closed questions, on the other hand, are restrictive and usually do not promote a dialogue.

Watch how open and closed questions can help you start conversations on your terms or focus on getting what you need.

> **Boss:** Charlene, you have a bad attitude; no, actually you have a lousy attitude.
>
> **Charlene:** Please describe what I did that you didn't like. (Open)

> ***Boss:***　You were very rude to that customer.
>
> ***Charlene:***　That wasn't my intent. What exactly are you referring to? (Closed)
>
> ***Boss:***　You refused to go out with him.

Charlene now has enough information to know that she is not willing to meet her boss's expectations. She can now ask another closed question.

> ***Charlene:***:　Is that one of your requirements for this job?

Depending on his answer, she can decide what to do next.

Charlene used a combination of open and closed questions to get all the facts she needed. In this case, she can introduce the subject of sexual harassment, or she can tell him that going out with a customer is not part of her job description.

Just asking these questions, however, is not enough if you want to be successful. Just as you erode your credibility with your body language, you unknowingly undermine and negate your own questions by inserting minimizing words or prefacing them with modifiers.

Do these patterns sound familiar?

"I just want to ask . . ."

"I'm only asking if . . ."

"This is probably a stupid question, but . . ."

"I was just wondering if . . ."

"Is it okay if I ask a question . . ."

"Would you mind if I . . ."

"Are you sure that I can . . ."

"Maybe if I . . ."

"I'm probably the only one who doesn't know this, but . . ."

Just reading these examples may make you cringe, because they remind you of how people belittle themselves before others even try to do it to them.

As if it's not enough that people often cloud their questions with words that make them sound weak and unsure, they then compound the problem with their tone of voice and inflection. Have you ever noticed how people's voices often take on an insecure quality, particularly when they lower voices and end sentences with an "up" tone or a giggle? Stop and think of all the messages that can be sent just by asking one question.

So, do be careful when you are asking questions. Make sure that your voice, your body language, and the content of your questions are all going in the same direction and sending the message you want the other person to receive. Questions asked effectively will not elicit defensive or aggressive responses. Directness or persistence: That's what you're aiming for.

POLITICALLY CORRECT CONFRONTING

Confronting others without alienating or angering them is an art. When done well, it is truly a thing of beauty, and when not done well, the details can be too gory to recount. If you are not willing to confront, it is probably because you've never learned how to do it, or you've never seen it done well. When even the most senior executives are asked which they would rather do, chew a piece of ice with a tooth that needs a root canal or confront someone face-to-face, 99.9 percent of the time they say, "Pass the ice."

Confrontation is a learned skill, and the good news is that it doesn't take long to become skilled at using it. It is really a feedback tool, designed to organize information so that the person getting the feedback or being confronted can hear it easily and, if possible, painlessly.

To help you position yourself so that you can confront logically and intellectually instead of emotionally and frantically, think about using the following model. It has actually changed the lives of a lot of people. This technique is not new and has been presented for a long time in many different formats. It is not lengthy or complicated, and when used properly it doesn't even seem like a technique, because it really is just a matter-of-fact way of organizing information.

To confront a difficult person—or any person, for that matter—organize what you want to say in five steps:

1. Give your perspective of the situation, as if you've taken a picture or a sound recording of their speech or behavior. The words to use are

   "When you . . ."

   This is also commonly known and used in many models for giving feedback. It enables you to give your observation of what your difficult person is doing or has done in a way that is descriptive and specific.

2. Give your understanding of what was said or done.

   "I understand this to mean . . ."

3. Describe what impact this had on you.

   "As a result, I . . ." or

   "This is (was) important because . . ."

4. State what you want regarding the situation.

   "I want to . . ."

   "My next step is to . . ."

Here is an example:

Your boss tells you that you are lazy, and you say to him, "When you said to me, 'You are lazy,' I understood this to mean that I had not done something you wanted me to do. This is important to me because I like this job, and I want to do it well, and I want you to tell me exactly what I didn't do and what you would like me to do now."

Quick, neat, and to the point. Here is another one:

Your significant other tells you that you don't care about what she wants. You say, "When you said to me, 'You don't care about what I want,' and you then slammed the door, I understood it to mean that you were angry at me and disappointed about my not doing something. This is important to me because I want to try to do what you want. I want you to tell me exactly what I did that gave you the idea I don't care about what you want."

Now look at how you might confront an unpleasant reaction from a difficult coworker:

"When I stopped at your desk and asked for your part of the written report that we are supposed to be working on together, you said to me, 'I'll get it to you when I'm good and ready.' I understood this to mean that you are not concerned about the deadline I have to meet to complete my part of it. This is important to me since we will both be held accountable for the quality and completion of the report. I intend to try to understand exactly what you are doing and go to our supervisor if you make it impossible for me to fulfill my responsibilities."

And here's how you might confront a doctor who you believe is dismissing you when you say that you don't feel well: "You said that my pain is all in my head and that I should take tranquilizers to help me calm down. I understand this to mean you are not willing to allow me to take the time I need to find out more about what may be causing the pain. This is important to me because my health and well-being are at risk. I intend to get a second opinion."

Sharp like a razor. Clear and direct. Now, you try one. Think of something that you want to confront. Make sure that it is something, not someone. Think about confronting the behavior or the issues, not the person. State it as succinctly as possible and then fill in the blanks. The biggest mistake that people make when doing this is to put step 2 material, interpretations, in the step 1 slot. Remember, to keep step 1 pure, think back to "Dragnet" ("Just the facts, ma'am") or Mr. Spock on "Star Trek"—unemotional detail.

Here are some other phrases that are handy for confronting:

When a person implies a threat but cloaks it ("I don't want to have to do something you might regret"), respond, "That sounded like a threat. Is that what you intended?"

If someone says, "A person like you is always causing trouble," ask, "How are you expecting me to interpret that remark?"

To an individual who says, "Your behavior surprises me," counter with, "What exactly are you trying to tell me?"

When a person loses his cool and you want to find out why, inquire, "If you had spoken instead of pounding the table, what would you have said?"

When your boss shortchanges you on your raise, ask, "How does the raise you are giving me relate to my performance?"

For the difficult person who says, "You know my answer, don't even bother to ask," follow up with, "What exactly are you saying no to?" Or: "Perhaps I wasn't clear. Please indulge me. In your own words, what did you hear me asking you to do?" Or: "What would it take to get a positive response from you?"

When you confront, you must be prepared to hear the answer the other person gives you. It may not be what you want to hear, and that probably makes it even more important. Unless you lay out exactly what you know the person is doing or saying and hold it up so that it is viewed the same way by both of you or all concerned, you will get suckered into an emotional spiral that will either deteriorate rapidly or accelerate into an attacking exchange. What you don't know can hurt you, and what you do know you can work on fixing and changing.

Once you tell the other person what bothers you; give your understanding of the situation; explain the reason that it is important to you; add your emotional response (or not); and articulate your plans, wants, or needs, you are giving feedback and confronting clearly. You can even go a step further and ask for the person's reactions, ideas, or commitment to work on the problem.

Some possible follow-up questions are

"What is your reaction to what I've just said?"

"Is there anything I've missed?"

"Are you willing to work on resolving this with me?"

If the person says, "Yes, I am willing to work it out," great! If the answer is no, you now know that you have a different issue to address.

Another method of confronting is to use contrasting statements. You begin with what you expected, wanted, needed, or understood would happen, and then contrast this with what you got or what actually did happen. It is important to be very specific when you do this.

Here are some examples:

"You told me that you would arrive by 6:00. You arrived at 8:30."

"Last week, you said that my raise would be 7 percent. The raise in my paycheck is 3 percent."

"You assured me that you would pay the credit-card bill by January 15. It is March 3, and there is still a balance of $800."

"I have told you eight times that my name is Judith. This is the ninth time that you have called me Jody."

"Last week, I asked you to tell me in private when you are displeased with something I've done. This morning you yelled at me in front of my coworkers."

The pattern is always the same. It is very specific, very factual, and very unemotional. Everything is divided into expectations or commitments and results.

If you want to become proficient in using these confrontation techniques, you need to practice. Many people find that the best method for learning these techniques is to talk to the steering wheel in their car, which is a good start, since it doesn't talk back or laugh. They then make their friends listen to what they want to say and how they plan to say it.

Don't think of yourself as imposing on your friends when you do this. In fact, it will be just the opposite. You'll be coaching and helping them as well. Make a day of it or at least a lunch.

PUTTING IT ALL TOGETHER: PROBLEM SOLVING

Throughout this book, it has been acknowledged that when you and a difficult person disagree, or when a challenging person does something you don't like, want, or need, you have a problem: The behavior is the other person's, but, alas, the problem is yours.

You can address each problem in such a way as to take it to its natural completion, and not go over the same issues repeatedly because you get tangled up and confused with heavy emotionalism. When you are angry or hurt, your thinking is not as clear as when you are calm, rational, focused, and relaxed. To compensate for this blip in your program, you need a systematic plan for streamlined problem solving. Here it is, five simple steps that will help you begin at the beginning, end at the end, and not take any unwanted, unplanned for, or unnecessary side trips.

STEP 1: Make sure you and your difficult person agree on exactly what the problem or the main issue is. To do this, use your listening, questioning, and confronting skills. If you can't reach consensus on this, you will never reach consensus on a solution.

You can use your second confronting technique here:

"This is what you said that you would do, and it didn't happen. To me, what's important is to find out what can be done now to remedy the situation."

Then ask:

"What do you see as the problem or main issue?"

Use your listening and clarifying skills here.

"Let me see if I understand. Are you saying that . . . ?"

State your desire to work on the problem or issue and ask if your difficult person is willing to do the same.

If the answer is yes, proceed to step 2. If it is no, go back to your questioning skills and find out why.

"You say you are unwilling to work on solving this problem. Help me understand the reasons."

If your difficult person doesn't want to talk about it, deal with it, or hear about it again, and you see neon lights flashing above his or her head that read, "Get used to it," you have to decide what you want to do next. Two options immediately come to mind. The first is to write the person off and work around him or her. The second is to give some reasons that would get the other person to take another look at the decision.

STEP 2:　If the person sees the light, move to this step: Each of you take a turn to describe what happened, how you got to this point, and what your choices are for solving the problem. Come up with as many possibilities as you can.

"What are all the different ways this problem could be resolved?"

Don't discard any ideas. Sometimes the best solutions come as a result of the most unusual suggestion. So make sure that you lay the ground rules, one of which is that it's not okay to say things like "that won't work," until you can test all the ideas for feasibility.

STEP 3:　Step 3 is just that, seeing which possible solution might fly.

"Let's look at the advantages and disadvantages of each idea and then choose the one that we agree is the best."

It is sometimes helpful to acknowledge your adversary's feelings.

"I know this is important to you. It is to me, too. That's why it's hard for me to do what we're doing now, asking you to join me in looking at something in a different way."

And at times, you may find it helpful to slip in a precondition:

"I'd be willing to go to your parents' house for Christmas after you come to mine for Thanksgiving."

The forced-choice technique that uses a closed question isn't really a great example of diplomacy, but it does deserve some mention since it gets to the heart of the issue:

"Which would you prefer, going to my parents' house for Thanksgiving or going to visit your family on Christmas alone?"

STEP 4: Choose the solution that sounds best and plan how to make it happen.

"Okay, who will do what, by when, and how will we know that everything is okay?"

This step introduces accountability, which is critical if you want to sustain long-lasting positive results. This is where the rubber meets the road, and the other person has to move from talk to action.

STEP 5: This is the "so-what" learning step, where you can acknowledge the positive outcome and plan for the next time there is a problem to work through.

"This really worked well. What can you and I do differently next time to take advantage of what we've accomplished?"

Now you have it, a no-frills problem-solving approach that is painless and effective. It combines a few of your new skills and can help get you through the murkiest of situations.

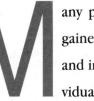

5

CONFLICT

SAVVY

Many people, once they've gained some new skills and insight, view the individuals in their lives who won't see things their way as fresh meat, and, as a result, they make the mistake of indiscriminately trying to apply everything they've learned all at once. Since difficult people are not all alike and the situations they create can be both complex and multidimensional, this is not recommended. To be effective at stopping them dead in their tracks, you have to be selective about what you do, how you do it, and, most important, when you do it. Positioning is everything.

When you try to confront or outthink the difficult people in your life without adequate preparation and forethought, you often inadvertently escalate the existing conflict and cause even more problems. Because you want to experience success and not fall into this trap, use this chapter to help you become conflict savvy.

THE LAST CHECK-IN POINT

But before you decide what to do when and when to do what, you have to decide whether to do it at all. So, before you get even more fired up, answer these questions about the person you are dealing with in your work situation:

1.	Have you decided that the behavior is truly unacceptable?	YES	NO
2.	Do you feel anxious every time you know you are going to see the person?	YES	NO
3.	Do you react negatively when you're with the person?	YES	NO
4.	Do you find yourself actually waiting for the person to be difficult?	YES	NO
5.	Is a relationship with the person important to you for social, emotional, or political reasons?	YES	NO
6.	Do you feel worse about yourself after you've spent time with the person than you did before?	YES	NO
7.	Do you want to change the way the person treats you?	YES	NO

8. If you never saw the person again,
   would it matter to you?   YES   NO

9. Does the behavior affect the way other
   people see or treat you?   YES   NO

10. If and when you've said something to the
    person in the past, was it turned around
    and used against you?   YES   NO

If you answered no to number 5, 7, 8, or 9, you would do well to reconsider whether you should deal with the person or change your situation altogether. If you answered yes to the other questions, you have indicated that you consider it important enough to address. Now you have to investigate just how much both of you see it as important and what both of your emotional investments will mean regarding what you do.

As has been said before, like it or not, your emotions get involved in your dealings with people. When you have a strong emotional investment, you have more at stake, so the decisions you make and the actions you take are much more important than they would be if you really didn't care very much at all. The same is true for the difficult people you deal with. The higher the stakes, the tougher the resistance they will put up, because they care more. You can use information about the degree of emotional investment you and the other party have to determine whether the time is right to deal with an issue, decide how you should position yourself, and assess whether the issue itself is important enough to be addressed at all.

Look at the following diagram. It has four squares: two pertain to your emotional investment, and two concern the cantankerous person's emotional investment. Each of the four combinations suggests a different plan of action.

The Emotional Investment Assessment

	I care	I don't care
The opponent cares	Not negotiable to me ① Not negotiable to my opponent	Negotiable to me ② Not negotiable to my opponent
The opponent doesn't care	Not negotiable to me ③ Negotiable to my opponent	Negotiable to me ④ Negotiable to my opponent

The best way to use these squares is to look at each of the combinations and decide which is most like the emotional-investment combination shared by you and your opponent or adversary regarding one of your problem issues. Based on your diagnosis, what, if any, steps would you take?

If square 1 describes your situation, you need to proceed slowly and cautiously. Since both of you have strong emotional investments, neither of you will willingly back off. Do your homework. Determine what motivates your opponent (chapter 2) and figure out a strategy to provide some of what is needed. Use questions to find out what's behind his or her emotional investment and use listening skills (chapter 4) to detect any hidden meanings or information.

If square 2 describes your emotional-investment combination, you are in particularly good shape, because you have some unencumbered alternatives. Regardless of the type of person you are dealing with, since you don't care much about the issue, you can take whatever action you want or score points by being giving. You also can decide to go after what you want and not be flexible. It depends on your past experiences with this person and what you're trying to accomplish. Use your feedback or step 1 of your confronting skills, feedbacking what you think the person wants and why it's important (chapter 4).

If square 3 is where you fit, you have to be a little more cautious. Since the person you are dealing with doesn't have a big emotional investment and you do (just the reverse of square 2), in this case, the other person is on easy street. Just because this individual doesn't care doesn't necessarily mean that he or she wants to share. You still need to position yourself so that you don't appear too anxious or vulnerable. Borrow some of the Logic Pusher's tactics (chapter 2), and prepare yourself with unemotional facts. It can't hurt to also know what category your difficult person falls into (chapter 2) so that you can make your pitch or react in a way that will get the best response.

Finally, the next stop is square 4, where the issue, in terms of emotional investment, is no big deal to either of you. This is a good place to be, because everything is up for grabs (except you, of course). Still, don't let down your guard too much; your difficult person might realize something along the way and change his or her mind and degree of negotiability, so prepare for it.

Don't let something go without enough thought to ensure that even if he or she did have a change of mind, the outcome would still be okay with you. In this case, ask yourself open questions (chapter 4) to really think it through.

Use this information to help you decide what to do when and when to do what. By assessing your different levels of investment, you can make a better choice regarding what, when, and how to act. Don't let the fact that you care erode your effectiveness.

WHEN TO SPEAK UP, WHEN TO CLAM UP

Knowing when and if to confront is almost as important as knowing how. There are certain situations that are appropriate and others that aren't.

Speak up when

1. You stand to gain more than you lose.
2. It's your job to say something.
3. You want to create an environment that reflects mutual respect.
4. You want honesty without hostility.
5. You don't want to condone future behavior.
6. You need to take care of your own interests.
7. You are not trying to teach the other person a lesson.
8. You are not preoccupied with flexing your own power.
9. You know the system will support your action.
10. You are not trying to make the other person look bad in order to make yourself look good.
11. You want to feel good about yourself and your behavior.
12. You have already unloaded and vented your anger far away from the other person, and now you are ready to talk about it.

A basic rule of thumb when deciding whether or not to take on a difficult person is this: If it makes a difference to you, go for it. If it doesn't, don't. Life is too short to sweat the small stuff. Ask yourself, "How will I feel tomorrow if I deal with the difficult person, and how will I feel tomorrow if I don't?" If it won't make a difference in your tomorrow, clam up. If it will, speak up.

Start with a basic question: Is your difficult person an introvert or an extrovert? That is, is this a person who is quiet or talkative? And why does this matter?

Whether such a person is motivated by need for power, admiration, or nurturing, dealing with him or her effectively means gearing your communication to the introverted or extroverted personality.

The introvert, it must be said, doesn't necessarily keep quiet to make you crazy, although sometimes it is a way of dealing with anger and displeasure. Introverts often hold back in order to blame you later for what you did or didn't do according to what they did or didn't want. Don't compensate for silence and withholding. In other words, don't keep talking for the sake of trying to force the other person to speak up. Acknowledge the silence. "I just asked you a question, and you didn't answer. I don't know how to interpret that." Or you could say, "If you had just answered my question out loud the way you undoubtedly did silently to yourself, what would I have heard you say?" These questions are not hostile; they are probing. Just make sure that you don't have a dagger on the end of your probe.

If you are an introvert and your difficult person is also an introvert, the one thing we don't have to worry about is one of you cutting the other one off in midsentence. In fact, you probably should be concerned about both of you using complete sentences. This may be an exaggeration, but two introverts are really not very likely to put issues out on the table unless things get pretty revved up. It's not that they don't feel, it's just that they don't tend to talk about how they feel. If you are an introvert, you can choose to keep your mouth shut or to open it, but when you don't open it, know that the other person can continue to act however he or she desires. Open your mouth when the time is right for you, not for the other person.

An extrovert is a very different animal. Not only does this person talk, but this person believes that people actually want and need to hear what he or she has to say. Extroverts exude, express, expand, spew, usually outtalk you, and often cut you off in midsentence. You have to be quick to get a word in edgewise with an extrovert. Extroverts don't hold back very well, and listening isn't often a strong suit. So, if you're an introvert dealing with an extrovert, take advantage of the fact that you might listen better than the extrovert does and be prepared to use what you hear (chapter 4). Extroverts do listen for one thing: their name. They always hear it, so when you want to get their attention, start by saying their name. Don't embellish it; instead of "Don, you jerk," just "Don" will do. Sprinkle the extrovert's name liberally throughout your comments, but be careful not to overdo. When dealing with an extrovert, make sure to provide a structure that will enable you to control what you say and at the same time persuade the extrovert to listen.

> "Don, I really am interested in what you just said, and
> I want to add two main points to your ideas. The first
> is . . . and the second is . . ."

You've just gotten the extrovert into the closed-mouth position, and you've reserved the person's brain for two points' worth of time. If you really want to excel, hold your hand in front of you, palm up, and raise two fingers counting off your points as you make them. This gives the extrovert some visual cues as well. This is not meant to be a sarcastic point. Visual cues help the extrovert to focus. Just make sure that your tone of voice is not cutting or sarcastic.

If you are an extrovert and the other person is an introvert, you've got some work to do in the self-control department. As an extrovert, you probably tend to try to take over whether you mean to or not, and this is not good. If you do all the talking, your introvert can just sit back and do nothing, and all you know is what you've said. You may also be affirming the introvert's tendency to not participate, providing the resistance he or she needs to maintain distance. So ask your question and close your mouth. Be prepared to wait in silence for an answer. If you don't get one, ask again.

Darlene, a definite extrovert, was on a road trip with Ted, a Self-Proclaimed Expert who was also an extrovert. This means that both of them could be outgoing, strong, and probably pretty pushy. At a certain point, Darlene knew exactly which freeway to take to get to their destination and so did Ted, or so he thought. He snapped at her when she said, "I think we should go north." As soon as she saw his reaction, she decided that it just wasn't worth it to argue. They were going to a function given by one of his friends, and if they were late, it would be his problem. She was just going along for the ride and to keep him company. She put aside her extrovert behavior, settled back in her seat, and waited for him to find out the hard way, which he did after driving twenty miles in the wrong direction.

On a subsequent trip, as soon as Darlene knew Ted was about to go the wrong way, she pulled out a map and said, "Would you like to check your route?" He looked at her, checked the map, and took the correct route. She didn't give him even one "I told you so." She had made her point, allowed him to come out looking good, and had avoided another forty-minute detour. It can be just that simple if you know who and what you're dealing with, you prepare in advance, and you are willing to change your style to fit the situation.

How to Make It Better

In every encounter you have with difficult people who you are trying to get to see things your way, until you become aware of your own behavior as well as what really makes them tick, you can hardly help making certain mistakes. These mistakes, resulting in the escalation of conflict, usually intensify the difficult person's feelings of anger and resistance to what you are trying to do.

A few tactics are particularly effective at de-escalating conflict. Keep these in mind and use them in combination with the other skills and techniques you are learning.

Try, when appropriate, to

1. Use humor. This is tricky, because although laughter can be the best medicine, it can also be inappropriate and offensive. Acknowledge your gut but listen to your head on this one.
2. Find common ground. Point out similarities instead of differences. There will be more discussion about this one in the forthcoming section on conflict routes.
3. Show willingness and flexibility. Don't come in with a chair and a whip (showing). You can always back up, and you will do better with flexibility.

4. Focus on one issue at a time. That's all anybody, difficult people or regular people, can do.

5. Be as factual as you can. Unless you have decided that this is a good time to try an emotional appeal, stick to a few solid facts and keep away from the fluff.

6. Show respect and empathy for the difficult person's position. Difficult people respond well to this approach, and it makes you look (and feel) really good!

Even when you feel yourself losing control or you change your mind about your desired level of participation in a given situation, you can always de-escalate the conflict if you

1. Keep your tone of voice consistent. Sound as natural as you can. If anything, lower your tone. Don't raise it.

2. Keep sarcasm for one-shot deals only. Like everyone else, difficult people forgive, but they don't forget. The after-effects of sarcasm will come back to haunt you in a long-term relationship, and the conflict shouldn't be about winning. It should be about resolution.

3. Make behaviors the issue, not personalities. Don't do a character assassination. It will really tick a difficult person off and, in the long run, work against you.

4. Don't make threats you're not willing to carry out. In fact, don't make threats at all. If you want to take action, just do it.

5. Don't adopt a superior attitude. Feel superior inside; sound strong and in control of yourself outside.

6. Don't stop listening. In fact, do just the opposite. Really listen carefully. The difficult person will love it and spill more beans than he or she ever intended.

To Escalate or Not to Escalate

How you initiate the discussion will either increase or decrease your difficult person's resistance to dealing with the situation. Here are some statements that escalate and some better alternatives that de-escalate.

Statements That Escalate
"We need to talk, because we have a problem."
"Don't you think that . . . ?"
"Why did you . . . ?"

Statements That De-escalate
"I think we should . . ."
"I want to talk to you about . . . ; it should take about five minutes." (Do not exceed fifteen minutes at first.)"
"Help me understand . . ." or "What were your reasons for . . . ?"
"Do you think that . . . ?"
"This is what I want to do. What do you want to do?"

You may often use the statements that escalate with the best of intentions to open up a dialogue and are surprised when instead of making things better, you've made them worse. The only time to use the escalation phrases is when you have cut your emotional investment and are going for broke.

You automatically escalate the conflict and unintentionally set yourself up as a loser whenever you use backfiring words like *because*—the kind of word that triggers justifying, defending, and explaining. It gets you tangled up in your own position. Ninety-nine percent of the time, even though you don't owe difficult people an explanation, it's hard not to "because" someone. Your Destroyer

Boss is demanding that you work overtime. "Sorry, I can't work overtime," you say, "because my child/wife/dog is expecting me." Now, your Destroyer threatens you with the idea that they'd go hungry if you had no job. So, replace this conflict-escalating statement with: "I'm not available to stay late this evening." Stop right before the "because" escapes your lips. Try to avoid overdefending your actions. If he demands an explanation, offer it courteously. Don't spew if it isn't necessary.

CONFLICT-RESOLUTION ROUTES

So that you can deliberately choose the best way to move through tough situations with difficult people, here are some routes to follow. This verbal road map may appear complex at first, but it's not. As you go through it one step at a time, think about how you might utilize each alternative.

Route 1: Do Nothing

This is like saying, "Leave well enough alone." You don't try to de-escalate or escalate the situation; in fact, you don't even let your difficult person know that there is a problem. When your difficult person is doing that difficult thing, instead of acknowledging it, you let it go. Not a bad strategy to use if there are people around, if you are so upset that you will totally lose it if you even open your mouth, or if you have a low emotional investment in the issue. You are choosing to withdraw temporarily or permanently. So you say nothing, and your difficult person doesn't even know that he or she has said or done something you don't like.

Carly works as a hostess in a restaurant. One night, a man came in and asked for a table. Since he had no reservation and the restaurant was full, Carly told him that it would be about forty minutes before he could be seated. In true Blamer fashion, the man chastised Carly, telling her in a loud and obnoxious voice that the wait was her fault because she wasn't doing her job properly. Carly looked at him, and all she said was, "Shall I put your name down on the waiting list?" Nothing more. She didn't change her tone of voice or take him on. There was no point, and since she was not the restaurant manager, she didn't have the power to refuse him service.

Route 2: Go for Broke

When you go for broke, you are engaging in battle with a might-makes-right approach. You are going for the win, hoping the other person will lose. It is an all-or-nothing move, and you can win big or lose big. You are imposing your position on the other; with this choice, even if you win, beware. Your opponent will probably try to get even, so although victory will be sweet, it may also be brief. But if you know that you are absolutely unwilling to abide by what the other person wants, this may very well be your best choice.

Art's boss wanted him to find some money in the budget for him to spend three extra nights in Las Vegas after his convention was over. He told Art to doctor the books so that no one would know. Art decided that he was unwilling to lie or do something dishonest for him and told his boss just that. He was ready for whatever consequences his assertiveness would bring; it was that important to him. (By the way, his boss got someone else to do it.)

Route 3: Let Them Have Their Way

This tactic means that you let your adversaries know that you disagree and want something different, and then go along with what they want anyway. You give in. It is an action that is sometimes referred to as the banking method of conflict resolution. You are making a deposit now, by giving in, so that later you can (try to) make a withdrawal, sometimes using guilt (see the "Below the Belt" section later in this chapter). Be careful though, because sometimes they will not recognize that you've opened an account, and when you try to get a payback, they may not pay. As discussed earlier, this is a good way to go when they have more of an emotional investment than you do.

June initially said no when Bob, her boss, asked her to drop off some material at a client's office on her way home. The problem was, she was in a hurry, and the client's office wasn't on her way home at all. She was supposed to get home early, because her brother-in-law was coming to dinner, and her boss knew this. Upon thinking it through, however, she realized that going out of her way to do this for her boss would accomplish two things. First, her boss would look good to the client, and, as an Admiration Hound, that was important to him; and second, getting caught in traffic would mean an hour less that she'd have to spend with her obnoxious brother-in-law. She told her boss that she'd changed her mind and that she would take the time to do it.

Route 4: Let's Make a Deal

This route requires that you split the difference. When you are willing to give other people some of what they want to get some of what you want, this is your move. It enables both parties to get at least a little bit, if not everything. What's good about it is that if you are at an impasse, you can both agree to do the minimum and move on.

Andy had a plumber come to his house to fix a pipe that had broken. Andy asked for an estimate, and the plumber did a "don't worry about a thing" number on him, which Andy allowed. When he was presented with a megabill, Andy just about flipped. After much discussion (the plumber said, "This is really cheap for what I had to do," and Andy countered, "I asked you to tell me how much it was before you started"), they split the difference. He still paid a little more than he knew the job was worth, but he had no more water on the floor. The plumber left with enough money for what he had done. Not a great outcome, but satisfactory.

Route 5: Work It Through

This is the two-heads-are-better-than-one approach. You don't try to convince or push another person to see it your way, and the other person doesn't try to convince or push you to do it another way. Together, you brainstorm and come up with a new solution to the problem that satisfies both of you. It is wonderful when it happens, but don't hold your breath. Both of you have to be willing to put your cards on the table and show your hands. You have to be willing to put your egos aside, really listen and understand what the other is saying, and clearly define the problem and go through all the steps (chapter 4).

John wanted to meet with Trisha on Wednesday at 5:30. Trisha had an afternoon meeting and wanted to meet in the morning instead. At first, they went back and forth, but once they each laid out their schedules for the day, they figured out that they could meet for lunch on Friday instead and it would work perfectly for both of them.

If you can, become familiar with all five conflict-resolution routes. These routes can be used alone or in combination, depending on what's needed to deal most effectively with your challenging people. You might choose to start by pretending it's not happening, and then when you're ready, move to putting it on the table and working it through. Use your own best judgment.

Don't just do what you've always done without examining whether there is a better choice. And if you make a poor choice, so be it. Have a postconflict discussion with yourself, your steering wheel, or a trusted friend, and prepare to do better the next time. Don't keep score; instead, keep trying. That's what conflict savvy is all about.

BELOW-THE-BELT TECHNIQUES

If you still aren't convinced that it's not okay to get down and dirty, this section will probably do the trick. Although what follows is delivered slightly tongue-in-cheek, it is nonetheless an important part of your conflict-savvy repertoire. Timing is everything, or close to everything, and a big part of timing is knowing when to pull out a totally different kind of behavior. In this section, you will learn about three: being helpless; pleading and groveling; and the creative use of guilt, the gift that keeps on giving. You could add a fourth, flattery, but it is so obvious that you just need to remember to not be above pulling it out when you need it. The decision to use any or all of these techniques is a very personal one. There will be times when you have to decide which is more important to you: being forthright or getting what you want.

Being Helpless

There may be times when the people you want to see things your way refuse to let you in. At such times, you could revert to nonproductive ways of operating. (You wouldn't have to tell anybody.)

Laura, an older employee, finds that many of the people in her company treat her like the "little old lady." At first, their condescension bothered her; she would get upset and resist. But she found out that confronting them made things worse. Now when she deals with these people, she really does act like a little old lady and happily reports that she gets more than she ever hoped possible.

Pleading and Groveling

As was said earlier, you can't talk about strategies for dealing with difficult people without giving pleading and groveling honorable mention at the very least. These strategies for what-to-do-when are rarely discussed in anything currently written about how to deal with difficult people. If you are a very assertive person, you do not normally use or consider these skills, but they do have their place.

Kate wanted her boss, Larry, to give her a travel assignment to Europe. Larry was best buddies with Ralph, who also wanted to go. Kate knew that there was no reason why Larry would give her the assignment, so when she began to feel Europe slipping through her fingers, she resorted to pleading and whining. She was relentless. Kate got the trip and made sure to drink a toast to Larry while sitting in a café near the Eiffel Tower. To her, it was worth it.

Not every situation with a challenging person is going to end with your getting everything you want; the law of averages is against you. Even though you may do the right thing at the right time in the right way, if the other person has a heavy investment in acting like the back end of a donkey—or in being "right," as he or she might put it—you just may not get a response to anything you try. If this happens (and you hope that it doesn't), you then have to decide how far you are willing to go to come out on top.

You get the idea. Appearing to act out of weakness will often get you what you want, but you have to

1. Really want what's on the table.
2. Do it for the sake of keeping your pleading and groveling skills primed and ready.
3. Want to see how far you can go with this technique.
4. Be pretty bored with the relationship.

The choice is yours. It has to be worth it to you.

What's Wrong with Guilt? It Works!

If you want to send a challenging or resistant person on a trip, it's fun every once in a while to make it a guilt trip. When conflict-resolution routes were discussed earlier, guilt was not included. Guilt has some connection to route 3, the letting-them-have-their-way option. It just takes it one step further and one step lower. Here's how it's done: You introduce the notion that you are going to give in and go along with what your difficult person wants; then you start laying it on thick. You make sure that your difficult person has a full understanding of everything you are giving up, the sacrifices you are making, the loss and inconvenience that you feel, and then, to add that certain *je ne sais quoi*, the fact that although your life or situation will be totally ruined, you're prepared for it.

Sending difficult people on guilt trips means helping them pack and making sure that they never forget how they got to where they are. When done well, making the opposition feel guilty can be a thing of beauty, enough to bring a tear to the eye. When done poorly, it can backfire, so be careful. Don't hesitate to use helpless facial expressions, the kind we rejected as not making you look assertive in the body-language section in chapter 4. In this case, you really don't want to look assertive. It's a delicate balance we're going for here: not too strong but not a total victim either. Make sure that your tone of voice doesn't sound sarcastic. Pay attention to how you end your sentences, and don't point at your difficult person with your trigger finger; it will cloud your guilt message.

Brenda wanted Jack to go out of town with her to a trade show, which was happening right in the middle of the World Series. Jack was an avid baseball fan and had tickets to attend all of the games with his longtime baseball buddies. Brenda reminded Jack about the free week in Maui that she had sacrificed for him. She then told him to "never mind," she would get one of the guys she worked with to go with her to the trade show because she knew that his games were more important than their relationship, anyway. Then, just for a little extra effect, she sighed one of those lingering sighs. Jack went to the trade show.

You have probably used guilt quite successfully yourself many times in the past. It is a good technique to have in your pocket, as long as you don't overuse it. Like pleading and groveling, it fills a niche. It is one more way to deal with resistance, and variety is the spice of life. But it definitely does not help if you want to build high trust and open, long-lasting relationships.

All of the ideas in this chapter work well, and the more adept you become at using them, the less of a chance the people who don't see it your way will have. Which brings you to an important and probably inevitable problem: backlash. Difficult people just may not stand up and cheer when presented with the more in-control and less explosive or vulnerable you; in fact, they may act out. So read on to prepare yourself to jump this one last hurdle.

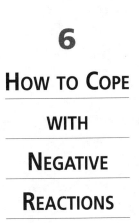

6

HOW TO COPE

WITH

NEGATIVE

REACTIONS

f you're a person who has always been in the background and rarely speaks up, never questions, and always complies, you can be sure that difficult people will have different reactions to your change of behavior. Some may say, "Hey, that doesn't sound like you. Are you having a bad day?" Others may continue to try to dismiss your opinions because you are not known as the type of person who seriously speaks up for what you want. They'll think that if they ignore you, your bad mood will blow over; and they'll get pretty nasty when they discover that it isn't a mood after all!

If, on the other hand, you realize that you have been getting in your own way because you have been speaking up too much or too aggressively, or you have been taking over inappropriately, any change in your behavior may be seen as an attempt at manipulation. This may also elicit negative reactions.

When you change your behavior, difficult people will have to change theirs. Many will find this inconvenient, more than likely resent it, and give you static about it. To help you understand that you have to look at the entire process rather than the immediate outcome, let's say you've always driven a car with an automatic transmission, and now, for the first time, you are learning to drive a car with a stick shift. At first, it's going to be a bumpy ride as the car responds differently to you, but eventually you are going to learn how to drive your new car effortlessly and automatically. People may not want to be in the same car with you at first; but in time they will get used to the idea, while you get better at shifting.

Learning to speak your own mind follows the same process. When you begin to shift your behaviors, difficult people are going to respond differently to you, and you have to expect that their reaction may not always be positive. The first time you say, "I'm not available to do that," and then don't feel obliged to give a reason, they may say, "What's the matter with you? You never used to be like this. You've changed." Using what you have learned in this book and speaking up come with some risk, but the results are well worth it, even though the reactions may be sweat inducing. You need to be ready when the backlash comes.

Backlash usually involves put-downs and testing on the part of difficult people who, as has already been said, are not necessarily thrilled with your new approach to them. This chapter will discuss two different ways to deal with what they dish out: slice and dice, and charm. Once again, depending on the difficult person, the situation, and your investment in it, you can choose which one will work best for you. Instead of separating them out, you'll get a chance to look at degrees of both. You'll begin with some different ways to say no, then you'll move to the pocket guide to responding to put-downs. From here, you'll go to dealing with testing, and, finally, how to deal for what you want.

It's Okay to Say No

As a newly emerging in-control-of-yourself, speaking-your-mind type of person, you will find yourself subjected to several unattractive verbal comments delivered by the pretty ticked-off, not to mention confused, difficult people who have been discussed. Threatened or inconvenienced individuals pull no punches, as you'll see in their responses in the put-downs section. They do whatever it takes to hang on to what they want. They say whatever they can think of to get their point across. If you tell a difficult person, "I am not going to cover for you. I have more important things I need to do," here are some of the destructive comments you might hear:

1. *The threat*: "Let me put it this way: if you don't cover for me, I'm not going to help you learn how to use the new software program that is being installed."
2. *The put-down*: "Do you really think that any other person would put up with someone as inconsiderate as you?"
3. *The put-off*: "I have no time for this garbage now; the meeting is starting."
4. *The denial*: "You're not too busy to cook for me. You just don't manage your time well."

5. *The cold shoulder*: "Quit whining. I know dozens of people who would trade places with you in a minute."
6. *The order*: "Just do it!"

This is just a sampling of what you might have to deal with. It is offered to get you in the mood for a technique you need to learn by heart, the technique of saying no.

It is okay to say no. You don't have to feel guilty about it. Nowhere is it written that yes is the only acceptable answer you can give a person who is giving you resistance. You have to be willing and able to set limits, even if it feels awkward at first.

Here's an example: You refuse to go to your significant other's class reunion. You've just gotten over the flu, you have a huge deadline coming up at work, and you desperately want to stay at home and take it easy. Your significant other reacts by getting angry and makes the same demand again.

How do you respond?

1. I'm confused. I thought we had resolved this, and I would hate to have it surface again and destroy our relationship.
2. What you're doing right now, bringing this issue up again, is making things worse.
3. I've made my decision.

Here's another example. Your boss tells you that important clients are going to be in town for the weekend and she wants you to entertain them. You get upset because she knows that you have to study for Monday's accounting exam. You have been working on your degree for two years now, and she knows how hard it is for you to find time to do all the work that is involved.

How do you respond?

1. You must have forgotten about the exam I have on Monday and how much time I need to prepare for it.

2. As much as I would like to, studying for my exam takes priority at this time.
3. As tough as it is for me to say no to you, I have to this time.

Don't underestimate the impact of each of the above choices; they are all very strong. Even though they are charming, they still say no.

Such a simple little word. Two regular little letters, but what power they have when they come together. Sometimes they have so much power that you have to soften them a little. The way to do it depends on how you want to come across.

Practice makes perfect. Try some of the following to get the hang of them. It's fun to watch the reactions difficult people have. You'll see confusion, surprise, horror, and who knows what else. Enjoy it! As a side note, these are also great to use when you get telephone solicitations at home at night, when you least appreciate them.

If you want to be	Make NO sound like this
Strong	"No. I am unwilling to do it."
Understanding	"I can see that this is a problem for you, and I can understand what you're going through."
Charming	"I really appreciate the opportunity you're offering me. Thank you. No!"
Noncommittal	"It sounds really great. Maybe next time."
Very definite	"Definitely not."
Enthusiastic	"I love that idea. Since I can't do it, I know that when you ask them, someone else will just jump at the chance!"
Disappointed	"I wish you had asked me yesterday, before I made another commitment."
Humble	"I'm flattered that you'd choose me. It won't work out, yet I appreciate your asking."

THE POCKET GUIDE TO RESPONDING
TO PUT-DOWNS

Now that you have gotten your feet wet in the no department, go a step further. There's a difference between saying no and responding to put-downs, which is what you'll get once you start saying no. When difficult people realize what's happening, they may say some nasty things. These can be insulting and demeaning, and many people have needlessly let themselves be destroyed by them. You can survive them and actually use them to your advantage.

Answering put-downs is better done in private, but sometimes you might need to do so in public. When this happens, a little humor can be really helpful in buffering the sting. The following put-downs are presented with a range of possible responses, some funny, some serious, and some with a tinge of sarcasm. The smaller your emotional investment is, the more likely you will be to use sarcasm. Look at each situation and relationship individually, consult your head, consult your gut, and proceed.

In addition, the following responses use some version of either the charm or the slice-and-dice approach. As you read them, see if you can find some that you would feel comfortable using. You can think up more of your own. Remember that your tone of voice and body language can make any message sound either charming or slicing and dicing and that slicing and dicing is very confrontational.

As you read through these, hopefully you were able to see a pattern. Most of the more caustic comments, though in all likelihood conflict escalators, are good for one-shot deals from which you can afford to walk away. The relationship-building responses, on the other hand, were geared toward either giving the difficult people specific information or engaging them to give you more information. This is just one more way to use the questions you learned about in "Getting the Information You Need Without Getting Their Goat" in chapter 4; and the more you use questions that are probing, the more information you'll have to help defuse the hostility you encounter.

When the other person says	You respond
You're too sensitive.	"I like that about myself. It makes me feel human." "Funny, it works for me." "Soft on the outside, crying on the inside, that's me. I like the fact that I'm consistent."
You're too emotional.	"I am not a programmed robot, and as a person with feelings, I will react. " "I am emotional because I have deep feelings about this." "My being emotional has nothing to do with it." "What would be different if I were less emotional?" "I am emotional because I care. Do you care?"
Lighten up.	"If I'm heavy, it's because I care a lot about this." "This is lighter; you should have seen me yesterday." "I'm light enough for me."
I didn't mean anything by it.	"Does that mean you'll never do it again?" "Does it matter to you that I didn't like it?" "What could you replace it with?"

When the other person says	You respond
I hug everybody.	"Am I the first person who has asked you not to?" "It's hard for me to tell you this, yet it is so important that I will. I feel uncomfortable when you hug me." "Except me, from now on."
If I didn't like you, I wouldn't say it.	"That's not how it sounds to me." "Somehow, this doesn't make me feel better." "What would you say if you *didn't* like me?"
If you liked me, you'd do something to help me look good.	"I wish it were that easy." "I don't see that as my role." "You are mixing two different issues." "You're right. If I liked you, I would." "Looking good is more important to you than it is to me."
Don't you think you should?	"Do you think I should? Oh, we disagree." "No, I don't."
Don't be so serious.	"My being serious means I respect what you're saying." "When I listen well, I get serious." "My 'serious control knob' is broken."
If I were you, I'd . . .	"I always enjoy hearing about the differences between us." "That does sound like something you would do." "I guess it's lucky you're not me."
You're the only one who . . .	"It isn't important to me to fit in." "I like feeling special and unique." "Once again, I'm a trailblazer. Is that a problem for you?"

When the other person says	You respond
Why are you making a big deal about this?	"I'm willing to spend time and energy on something that is important to me." "What would you prefer I do?" "Why are you?"
I haven't got time to talk about it now.	"Are you willing to make the time since it is very important to me?" "When will you have time? Tonight or tomorrow morning?" "You don't have time to not talk about it."
Have you gained a little weight?	"Is my weight of interest to you?" "I would prefer to talk about something else." "Let's talk about you instead of me."
That was a dumb thing to say.	"If you were saying it, what would have been different?" "Is it different from what you wanted me to say?" "I'll try to say it differently."
Boy! That was stupid.	"Does 'stupid' mean that you disagree?" "What were you hoping for?" "What specifically is it you don't like?"
I can't believe you said that.	"What specifically are you referring to?" "Is there something in particular that you are having trouble with?" "Believe it. I said that."
I can't believe you would do that.	"Is it different from what you wanted me to do?" "What can I do to clarify what I did?" "Believe it. I would."
Do you know how many would kill to be in your position?	"Are you asking whether I appreciate people like you?" "They're desperate. I'm above that."

When the other person says	You respond
You're not happy unless you're making my life miserable.	"Making your life miserable is not my intent." "What, specifically, are you referring to?" "I'm sorry you feel that way."
What makes you so special?	"Do you really think I'm special or are you being sarcastic?" "A lot of things." "How much time do you have?"
(The other person says nothing but rolls her eyes.)	"You just rolled your eyes. What does that mean?" "If you had spoken instead of rolling your eyes, what would you have said?" "Do you have something in your eye?"
What happened to the enthusiastic person I hired?	You turned him into me. I must seem really different to you right now. If you let me out of your office, I'll go look for her.

How to Deal with Testing

Aside from biting comments, what other kinds of behavior can you expect from difficult people struggling to hold on to what they have? It depends a lot on the intensity of their reaction to your new approach to dealing with them. If they feel threatened, they may lash out and become (more) obnoxious, or they may withdraw and use more passive or passive-aggressive behaviors. An introvert may become more verbal, and an extrovert might become more so or much more low-key. In any event, one thing is inevitable: There will be a testing phase. Testing is merely an extension of the denial your difficult people will experience because they don't want to accept the fact that they can't go home again. This relates back to what was talked about in chapter 3: The party is over and the rules have changed.

Some difficult people may actually worry about their power as a result of your newfound strength. When you threaten this part of their ego, their reactions might be interesting, to say the least, and they may feel compelled to test you to see how they stack up against the new you. They may also test you to see just how far they can go and how much they can still influence you. They may feel compelled to check your Deference Quotient.

Most adversaries are very transparent. It is easy to determine if their issue is control, acceptance, intellectual dominance, emotional security, egocentricity, or anything else. The way they test you will expose their motives.

Gloria deals with testing at the office. When the issue of sexist language comes up, everyone looks to her, because she is responsible for cleaning it up and getting the men to change their vocabulary. "Traditional terms like 'man hours' or 'we have to man the booth' are something that the men I supervise don't want to give up. When they use such terminology, I always smile first and then say, 'staff hours' and 'staff the booth.' And they say, 'Come on, no one minds "man" in these situations.' To which I answer, 'Would you like to start calling it "woman hours" and "woman the booth"?' When they laugh and say, 'We wouldn't mind,' I laugh and tell them, 'So do it.' And then they say, 'staff hours' and 'staff the booth.'"

It's difficult for people to change their habits, and so they will keep testing to see how many they can keep. Gloria often tries to use humor. "Sometimes they groan and roll their eyes and I just smile my best smile, and they groan once more and give in. At my level, the put-downs I get are generally done with humor. Difficult people wouldn't dare to take me on face-to-face without a lot of humor, so I'm able to respond in kind. The messages are clear."

Humor is an important part of the charming approach. It can lighten up a potentially heavy and uncomfortable situation. Many women have found that in any male-dominated situation at work, they have to start by proving themselves and their ability to do the job and take what men dish out. Having done that, then they are able to joke and be charming. The reason? Men are then ready to recognize women as people, rather than as just women doing a previously male-defined job. It is a given: Women who work in a male environment will be tested on their qualifications and their personalities. Once men know women can do it, they stop challenging and start relating.

Greg's coworker, Dick, was known to swear and had no respect for anybody or anything except his own boss. As a result, when he disagreed with anyone else's decisions, he would yell and curse at them. One day, Dick telephoned Greg and began screaming, "I just heard your decision on . . . What the hell is wrong with you? Do you have rat droppings for brains? There's no way in hell that I am going to let BS like this happen!"

At which point, Greg thought to himself, "Who does he think he is? I'm not going to take this abuse." So Greg said, "If you've got a problem, tell me what it is and I'll listen. Then, I'll discuss it with you. If you think you can call and curse at me over the telephone, you're wrong. I'll hang up. Never call and curse at me again." And he never did. Dick pushed as hard as he could to see where he could go, and he got his answer: Nowhere.

Flight attendants who work in first or business class, where it seems as though difficult people are almost the only type admitted, are usually experts on being charming and dealing with testing. Granted, they don't always deal with backlash, but they do get the brunt of whatever these difficult people have been up against all day. And because of their position, flight attendants are just expected to take it and back down.

Larry's approach is simple: "I treat them as if they are little children in grown-up bodies. That way, I know just what to expect, which is not much, and how to deal with them, which is easy. I treat them like children—with respect, but like immature people who haven't been socialized to know how to behave."

Carla takes it one step further: "Since I know I can outthink and outsmart them, I make a game out of seeing how long it takes to get them right where I want them, in the palm of my hand."

For a long time, Joel worked on commuter flights heavily traveled by people who had been wheeling and dealing all day. As a result, they were often downright nasty by the time they boarded the plane. He explained his tactics this way: "Early on, I learned to pick out the people with the tight jaws and the most tense expressions, so that when they sprang into action and started making demands and yelling at me, I was ready with my most sympathetic 'I want to please you' manners. One of my best responses has always been 'I hope I can make your day better, as of right now.' I'm not in a power play with these difficult people. I just want to make sure that they don't feel compelled to act out in order to prove themselves to me. I charm them into submission." Difficult people can be like big babies. When they lash back because they don't get their way, you really can deal with them. Watch for clues so that you can head them off; sometimes all it takes is a smile, at other times a little teasing. Charm and grace under pressure go a long way.

Mark is a very successful former actor who is now active in business and interacts with very powerful people. "I never put them on the defensive. The most important lesson I've learned is to defend myself without attacking. I try to be polite and charming, with impeccable manners. I've learned to communicate my thoughts as clearly as I can. I've found that they may not come over to my way of thinking, but if I'm courteous, at least they'll listen, and that's half the battle. That's the way I have many more victories than defeats. My brand of charm often includes humor. I can say almost anything with a friendly laugh and get my point across. I don't go for the jugular. I don't have to prove anything."

How do older and more experienced people test younger, but sometimes more highly paid, people? They probe the outer limits of their knowledge and skill by asking a lot of questions, posing problems, and pushing to find out how theoretical situations would be handled. Then they watch to see how the younger workers cope with adversity, whether they become "too emotional," and how much of a good sport they are. They wait to see whether they blame others or are team players. In many workplace situations, the more experienced workers want to see if the younger workers have been given jobs that they were not ready for, because some of them have fallen apart doing them and then have been banished from other key positions because they "weren't cut out to be in the trenches." Those who are not impetuous, but who are in control, not mean, and able to laugh at themselves will get through the testing phase and graduate to being accepted.

In dealing with backlash, what complicates matters is that slice-and-dice and charm are just a voice inflection, facial expression, or hand gesture away from one another. To do either well, you have to pay attention to the skills discussed in chapter 4 and the conflict guidelines reviewed in chapter 5.

You have to be prepared to deal with put-downs by either ignoring or responding to them. You have to be willing to say no in whatever manner feels right to you at the time; you have to be ready to deal with and endure the testing that will eventually occur; and you will do yourself a favor if you anticipate ways in which you can strike deals for the behavior you want from difficult people.

The toughest change you will have to make as you deal with backlash is overcoming the tendency to back down—to say that you didn't mean anything by what you said or did and to decide that it's not worth it and that you'll just do what you've always done. Backlash can be very draining; it can wear you down, but do whatever you have to in order to stand firm. Pop some extra vitamins. Get a telephone support buddy or coach. Whatever works for you. There is too much at stake for you to risk caving in, no matter how many times your nemesis asks you to cover and take the blame for him at a meeting or to not say anything when he makes a mistake. Practice in advance.

There is a funny definition of insanity that you may have heard that is relevant here. Insanity is "doing the same thing over and over again, but expecting the results to be different." Difficult people will keep on testing and hoping that even after you have begun to use your new skills, you will change your behavior back to what it was.

Or, as Brenda says, "Face it; all difficult people are like frogs, and I don't plan to accept the position of lily pad again any time soon."

7

GET USED
TO SUCCESS

t is not always easy adjusting to relationships with people who formerly did not see it your way. Whether you are dealing with your boss, your coworkers, your friends, your family, or your significant other, the one thing that you will notice is that the dynamics of each relationship will definitely be different. You may feel pressured to take more responsibility for keeping your relationships open and honest. You no longer have an excuse for acting like a victim or a warrior when they resist what you want or are asking them to do. As in a tug-of-war, when the difficult person stops tugging, you have to stop as well or you'll fall flat on your face. Once you know how to bridge the communication gap between you and another person, the only thing left for you to do is to utilize your skills and awareness to make sure that you stay on a constructive, although not necessarily easier, path.

You need to be prepared to give up your anger and frustration and replace it with a sense of enjoyment and accomplishment. After spending some time thinking about what it will take for you to break some of your old habits, hopefully you now realize that even though the mind-set that you've been in may have been comfortable, it has been nonproductive for the most part. By improving your skills and style of communicating and getting what you want in your relationships, you will now be prepared to manage your relationships instead of being managed by them. Can you let go of the hostility and the resentment? Here are a few last-minute adjustments to help you do so.

DEFERENCE SYNDROME RECOVERY— ONE DAY AT A TIME

The focus throughout this book has been about the various processes involved in dealing with difficult people who don't want to or just plain can't see things your way. It has stressed the fact that, regardless of the situation you are in, there is always another way to approach what is happening by approaching the other party. You already may have begun to try out some of the techniques presented to change your attitude and behavior, and the other person may have begun to change as well. Can you stop reading now? It's probably not a good idea. You have narrowed the gap, but you have not sealed it airtight. Change that happens overnight rarely sticks. It takes a lot of reinforcement and repetition to internalize and integrate anything really different from what you have been doing for a long time. People (men and women, difficult and otherwise) often attend a one-day seminar and by the end of the day are chomping at the bit to change their worlds. Sometimes it is almost necessary to block the door so they don't leave and head straight for a major letdown. If you, like these people, have this urge, no one can block your exit, so to speak. However, you can stop and remind yourself of the importance of proceeding slowly.

You may have unknowingly suffered from Deference Syndrome for a long time. It may have shaped your world to a great extent and influenced who you are, what you do, and those with whom you do it. And now, hopefully, even though you have just read this book and just begun to think about adjusting your attitude, it will not behoove you to try to overhaul all your old beliefs and subsequent behaviors at once. Don't expect to go from a moth to a butterfly in microwave time. Don't look at every person as a potential assertiveness exercise; it would be too exhausting for you and for them. Don't turn into the consummate charmer, either, or you will have difficult people everywhere, either laughing or ignoring you because of the extremes in your behavior.

As much as you may dislike the word *moderation*, this really is a good time to bring it up. Just because you're reading the last chapter of this book doesn't mean you're finished. Far from it. You do have an excellent chance of permanently changing the dynamics of your relationships with people who, up until now, haven't wanted to see it your way, but if you do it too fast, you will tick them off, put them off, confuse them thoroughly, or behave in a way that you may not be willing or able to sustain.

By now you have a lot more options available to you. You have learned about several techniques involving communication and confrontation and have had an opportunity to begin the process of adjusting your self-esteem (upward).

You now know that if you have suffered from it, you will finally be able to overcome Deference Syndrome because you have changed the way you look at difficult people, yourself, and the situations in which you find yourself. By the same token, you now hopefully feel much better about yourself knowing that you are but one of many who have doubts about their ability to turn a bad situation around. You have exchanged blame for planning and self-consciousness for curiosity. You have decided that you don't have to be as tough as nails or as soft as a marshmallow. You realize that there is a lot of latitude in how you can successfully approach and deal with tough people in even tougher situations.

If you did suffer from Deference Syndrome, take a few minutes now to reflect on the major beliefs you have now rejected. When you believed that you had to be deferential to a given person, what did it entitle that person to say to you and about you? What did it entitle that person to do to you or about you? What did it say or mean about that person's intelligence in relation to yours?

If you really don't hold those old beliefs anymore, the next part of your recovery should be a real snap!

People have their own methods of setting themselves up for failure in dealing with difficult people. Either they expect too much of themselves or they expect too much of difficult people. Again, to keep you going after the initial rush of your jump start has subsided, it will be important for you to give yourself some positive reminders, regardless of the ups and downs you are experiencing on a day-to-day basis. Here are some suggestions. Read them and add a few of your own.

The Deference Syndrome Recovery Reminders List

1. I can cope with anything thrown my way.
2. I have a lot of good ideas that I can put into practice.
3. I have to expect that I will screw up some situations.
4. I have a lot of power, and I can choose whether or not I want to use it.
5. I don't have to prove anything to anybody.
6. I deserve the best I can get. I am that important.
7. I create my own reality. The best way to get positive relationships is to create them myself.

Now, add some of your own:

8.
9.
10.
11.
12.

Put this list where you can see and get to it easily and read it every day—twice a day when you have to deal with people who don't want to see it your way.

HOW TO AVOID BACKSLIDING

When you begin taking better care of yourself and enjoying the fruits of your labor, you won't want to backslide. Your desire, however, may not be enough to keep you going forward, especially if you are dealing with sporadic backlash. In addition to using your reminders, you'll need to have a plan, an agreement that you make with yourself to make sure you stay on track. In implementing your antibacksliding plan, ask yourself—and answer—these four questions:

1. What difficult behavior am I going to deal with?
2. What exactly am I going to do?
3. How am I going to do it?
4. What resistance should I prepare for?

If you don't short-circuit backsliding and stop it before it starts, you might end up like a case of boiled frog. Sound disgusting? It is disgusting, and here is why. It is a well-known though slightly esoteric fact that if you put a live frog into a pot of boiling water, it immediately knows that it is not in a good place. As a result, it immediately tries to jump out of the water. If you put the very same frog into a pot of cool water and gradually turn up the heat to the boiling point, the frog will do nothing except go to sleep.

There is a good reason for telling you this. There is a logical connection. If you have a blatantly horrific experience with a difficult person, it will keep you on your toes and on the case, as it were. But if you have instances of little or no consequence, and you let them pass without ever evaluating your overall strategy, it won't be long before you're back in the same old rut or pot. So don't snooze in a pot of lukewarm water. Expect positive experiences and you'll create them.

Backsliding conjures up an image of a person sailing backward down a long metal chute, hopefully with some padding on the rear end so that there is no bruising on landing. If you don't want to put yourself in this picture, make sure that you don't make the ten most common mistakes that lead to backsliding:

1. Don't become too cocky. Difficult people are amazingly creative. Just because you've seen one routine doesn't mean you've seen them all.

2. Don't be afraid to ask for help from a friendly source. I always suggest starting a support group in which other people who are also trying to change their behavior and situations can coach each other.

3. Don't discount all people who don't want to see it your way as difficult. They're not. A lot of these people are just trying to do their jobs and have no hidden or destructive agendas. You might be able to gain insights from them.

4. Don't broadcast the "new you" to the world. Many individuals make the mistake of boasting or bragging to anyone who'll listen. Resist the urge. Congratulate yourself quietly.

5. Don't think that once is enough. Remember the testing practices of difficult people, who test to determine how much they can get away with and to discover exactly what it would take to undermine your new attitude and behavior. Prepare yourself for repetition.

6. Don't get so caught up that you carry the banner for all people who feel the same way as you. You'll burn yourself out if you try to take the Robin Hood approach.

7. Don't expect to be liked and heralded by others for taking control of yourself. Some of these people may feel threatened, and others, still suffering from Deference Syndrome, may resent you for rocking the boat.

8. Don't forget to acknowledge the progress you make, even if it isn't monumental. Just put one foot in front of the other and appreciate that you are moving forward.

9. Don't stop trusting yourself. If you take action that doesn't quite work out as you had hoped, don't begin to doubt

your gut or your intellect. Difficult people are not machines, and they don't always do what you expect.

10. Don't worry; start working. Decide to continually upgrade your how-and-what-to-do-when skills. There is always something new to learn.

Taking responsibility for improving the situations with the difficult people in your life can be very exciting and rewarding. If you have a plan and you execute that plan, you get to do one of two things: enjoy your success or plan for the next time with a lot more experience under your belt. It was said earlier and is worth repeating: It is up to you to bring these ideas to life, to allow them to work for you as you get stronger and more competent. Take the time and make it happen.

Another method that you might find useful is to have a two-way conversation with yourself. There are a lot of jokes about people who talk to themselves, but often it's a great idea. It is the ultimate control experience. You get to ask the questions and give the answers. If you feel yourself backsliding or backing away from the plate instead of stepping up to it, ask yourself (and then answer) these questions:

1. What exactly am I trying to accomplish?
2. What makes it important to deal with it at this particular time?
3. What is my plan?
4. What will it look like in action?
5. What will I get from using it?
6. What are my concerns?
7. What reactions might I get?
8. Have I planned well for resistance or backfires?
9. Is it worth the risk?
10. How will I feel after I've done it?

After you've answered these questions, put them aside for a little while and then go back to them. Give yourself some time to become slightly more objective, before reading what you've written. Make any changes you think valid or necessary, and give yourself a pat on the back for keeping the momentum going in the right direction.

ENJOYING NEW RELATIONSHIPS WITH PEOPLE WHO ARE BEGINNING TO SEE IT YOUR WAY

Recall when you first started reading this book. At that time, when you thought about dealing with the most resistant and challenging people in your work life, how would you have rated yourself on this "Dealing with People" Anxiety Scale?

0	1	2	3	4	5
cool as a cucumber	very slight anxiety, anger	mild anxiety, anger	moderate anxiety, getting nervous, anger	pretty nervous, beginning to panic, anger	over the edge, fear, anger

And now, rate yourself after reading this book. Each stage of this scale is typical of what individuals go through during their approach to dealing with difficult people who don't want to or can't see it their way. It's amazing what a little knowledge and confidence can do. With practice, you can make sure that you remain at the lower end of the scale. In fact, you are probably pretty close to erasing numbers 3, 4, and 5 already. Number 2 will go after you've had a few more positive experiences. There is no mystery to it. Practice makes as close to perfect as you can get. You will in fact find that in your new and improved dealings with challenging people, you will trade insecurity for respect, and, in many cases, it will be mutual. Both of you will become more secure, and both of you will respect yourselves and each other a lot more. At home, Louie told his wife, "If you will step back and give me a chance to be who I want to be, I think that you'd like me a lot more." She did, and she does. At work, Louie asked his boss to give him a chance to do a project his way, saying that he would redo it if his boss didn't like the end product. He did it his way, and his boss was pleased. Sure, sometimes you will be lucky to arrive at minimal tolerance, because there are always a few holdouts, but don't underestimate your newfound power.

In reading this book, you have hopefully taken the time to step back and think about and remember people and situations that were destructive to you, your career, and your relationships. In the past, you have no doubt laughed, poked fun at, and thought critically about a lot of the difficult people who have passed through and continue to pass through your life. It may have been a way of protecting yourself from more anger, hurt, and frustration. You have more options now. You can acknowledge your feelings and think your thoughts as long as you then move forward and do something constructive about them. You can handle it. You know how to be tough, you know how to be factual, you know how to be charming, and you know how to engage. Face it, you know what to do—you just have to do it.

The world of people who don't yet but soon *will* see it your way is your oyster. The next time a person tries to take you on, ignores what you say, or tries to put you down before or after you open your mouth, take a moment to focus. Consider the choices that you have and what you want to accomplish. You will remain in control of the most important person in this equation—yourself. You can then relax and enjoy putting your new skills to work.

INDEX